contents

acknowledgements

___

The authors would like to thank the following for their help:

Michele Bunn, State University of New York, Buffalo

Hubert Crowther, BMR

Colm Donlon, IDA Ireland

George W. Dudley and Shannon L. Goodson, *Earning What You're Worth? The Psychology of Sales Call Reluctance*, Behavioral Sciences Research Press Inc.

Kevin Geaney, Plastic Services Kolthoff Ltd

Journal of Marketing

Marketing News

Maurice McMonagle, Siemens

Michael Nolan, Sheppard Moscow

David T. Nourse

FKI Plc

John E. Schorr, *Purchasing in the 21st Century*, The Oliver Wright Companies

introduction

---

the shut-out

Ever tried banging your head against a brick wall? It hurts! Yet so often, day in day out, salespeople, marketers and business development executives persist in going through this process. It's as though they have run down a dead-end alley and are confronted by a brick wall. There's no hammer and chisel to help them through, so they bang their head against the wall. Eventually they leave the scene battered and bruised. It hurts!

Getting access to buyers can seem like banging your head against a brick wall. You call, they're in a meeting. You call again, they're off-site. You get a buyer on the line, he's disinclined to meet you. You send a brochure and spec and follow up with a call. He's still disinclined to meet you – he already has three preferred suppliers. You get to arrange a meeting and drive 150 miles to see him, but he's forgotten, or had a crisis and had to go off-site. You eventually get a request to quote on some small business, but you're way out on price. Every contact is a knockback. *Life* is a knockback! That's the shut-out.

A salesperson chases one lead after another. Her only remit is to secure business from wherever possible. The product she's trying to sell doesn't really satisfy the needs of the buyer. She's unfocused and becomes disillusioned. The only consistency is the number of rejections. It hurts! It's the shut-out – the brick wall, the closed door, the unanswered phone call, the binned letter.

A quotation request is treated with suspicion because the demands for information seem excessive. The management is fearful or suspicious. 'Is there anything the buyer doesn't want to know?' is the sarcastic question. The salesperson's hard work is to no avail. He's even shut out by his own side's lack of effective support!

Many salespeople and marketers blame themselves if they lose a contract, a bid or an account. Yet the reason for the knockbacks, rejections and shut-outs may have absolutely nothing to do with their efforts, their personalities or the quality of interpersonal contact they have with their prospects or regular buyers.

Within business-to-business markets the skill and professionalism of buyers is continuously improving. The continuing professional development of the purchaser is in danger of leaving the marketer behind, making the selling and marketing effort ever more difficult. Nowadays the answers to successful contract negotiation lie far beyond personal selling and good operations management. They are hidden in the market structure and the strategies adopted by the target buyers.

This book can help the salesperson/marketer to strike back, whether he or she is selling to retail multiples, production buyers or through distributors. We believe it will interest consumer marketers and salespeople who are looking for a different, more difficult (and, we believe, more exciting) challenge, and also interest people working outside of sales and marketing who want a good grasp of how business-to-business marketing can work.

As with every difficult challenge, there are no easy answers. However, there are four things which can make a significant difference to people doing business with professional buyers:

● know the market better than the buyers do

● have a workable business plan with specific actions programmed in

● exceed the buyer's expectations

● think relationships as well as deals, orders and contracts.

Chapter one looks at 'taking the market apart'. This means developing an accurate reading of what's actually going on in the marketplace, helping to out-think the buyer. This book takes to heart the idea that in order to sell or market, you need to understand the customer, the buyer, the person who really drives your business. Consequently, chapters two to four deal with buyers – how they organise, how they operate, what their priorities are and where the sources of their power lie. Chapter two takes a look at the 'buying function' as it is structured in a modern organization. Chapter three takes a look at the many stages in the 'buying process' and what actions may be suitable for the sales/marketer at each stage. Chapter four deals with 'buyer power' as well as buyers' general requirements and includes a special section on the buying and selling of manufacturing tools, an area that is often neglected.

To pull the analysis together and develop an integrated response to the complex challenge of managing relationships with key account buyers, chapter five cuts through the often over-complicated verbiage of objectives and strategies and integrates the main aspects in a simple business planning framework. Finally, chapter six introduces the 'buyer relationship framework', a seven-point practical framework for handling business with key buyer accounts.

Julian J Gibas
Daragh O'Reilly

1

taking the market apart

In creating relationships with buyers it is essential to be absolutely clear about what you're getting into. In fact, ideally you need to read the market better than the buyers! By taking the market apart according to the simple framework in this chapter, you can out-think them!

introduction

In order to out-think professional buyers, it pays to understand the market better than they do. They start with a huge advantage, in that they know your competitors' capabilities in much greater detail than you can ever hope to do. But if you focus on the bigger picture and learn to read the way the market is going, this can be a significant counter-advantage. Because their jobs are so pressurized and focused on detail, often they can't invest the time in looking at the strategic picture. In this way they resemble salespeople who are so busy chasing leads and making sales calls that they cannot step back and see where all the rushing is taking them.

○ *Give yourself a break!*

○ *Take some time out.*

○ *Check out what's really going on in your market!*

TRICKS OF THE TRADE

In order to find out how something really works, you take it apart and work out the inner connections. Markets are no different. This chapter gives you a framework for taking any market apart.

PBA – paralysis by analysis?

In conducting a rigorous appraisal of its operating environment, there's a risk that an organization will become afflicted with PBA – paralysis by analysis. This phrase is often on the lips of 'action people' who like to 'get things done'. Beneath the 'just do it' machismo, however, lies the fear they are trying to hide. The full picture is often too complex and too difficult for them to grasp, so they remain stuck in 'doing things' (usually the way they've always done them).

○ *Well, the world's changing, and changing fast. There's no room or use any more for people who are too stuck, lazy, scared or unimaginative to look at the full picture.*

○ *There's too much money and too many people's jobs at stake to ignore the need for analysis. Action should not be a substitute for thinking.*

The benefits of not analyzing the market are a misplaced sense of comfort and the illusion of knowing all the answers. It's often painful discovering new things about oneself that one didn't know – the real truth. If the company assumes all the time that it knows what its customers, bankers, stakeholders, employees and suppliers think, that feels comfortable. Analysis, however, means extra work and learning the hard facts about other people's perceptions about the company.

If the company doesn't understand how the market really works, then how can it have an effective strategy? Many companies cannot face the hassle and aggravation of collecting data. They give up, because they expect it to be easy. Perhaps they have the naive belief that their competitors will open up their hearts and disclose their closest guarded secrets in one swift phone call. Sadly, life's not like that!

Better to be paralyzed by analysis – at least the data is there – than zombified by ignorance!

FAST TRACK

EXAMPLE

Racal Electronics takes the market apart

Racal Electronics was looking at ways in which to expand its American market within the passive infra-red household and commercial security sectors. It visited the International Fire and Safety Exhibition at the Jacob Jacovitz Centre, New York, where it was able to identify potential users and producers of security systems. It came across plenty of anecdotal evidence suggesting that wireless security systems represented a growth sector.

Wireless systems were reasonably cost effective to produce and the ease of installation far outweighed the complexity of wiring-in a traditional system. There was a possibility that wireless systems could have their signals jammed or blocked, but this would be very difficult to achieve.

Racal's market research coincided with the Federal Communications Committee releasing new frequencies to be used for security systems. This further whetted its appetite and Racal concluded its market research by talking to security systems suppliers and distributors.

This research confirmed the anecdotal evidence which Racal had originally picked up from the exhibition. It very quickly established a presence in the marketplace as one of the leading suppliers of wireless security systems and developed a multi-million dollar business.

Racal heard of an opening, took the market apart and went for it. ○

point of view

Whenever someone is conducting an analysis, his or her point of view is important. The analysis of a market context can be undertaken by an individual simply to gain the increased personal insight this exercise brings. The new angles generated can be used to enhance personal performance at internal or sales meetings.

An analysis carried out as a project by a group of executives working together can produce even more new ideas, as different points of view are brought to bear on the focus of attention. The framework proposed in this book can be used in either setting – the individual or the group.

analysis made easy - the five Cs

Analysis is simple if you have a convenient framework. When working out what makes a market tick, whether it's the treasury market, the submersible pumps business, passenger jet leasing or the demand for specialist workstations, you need to focus on just five things – the five Cs:

- context
- customers
- competitors
- critical success factors (CSFs)
- company

context

Context means the product-market, the business, the game you're in and the environment external to the organisation. How you define your business context or competitive domain can have significant repercussions for your business success. So this needs to be treated with care.

Before you can work out where you are, what's going on and what to do about it, you need a map of your area. To help draw that map, you need to decide what business context you are operating in.

WHAT BUSINESS ARE YOU IN?

Many people define their business with reference to the products they manufacture or services they provide. While these are major determining factors, relying on a product or service description alone can be dangerously misleading. In practice, a thorough examination of the question is worthwhile, as it can lead to new insights about what customer needs the business is trying to meet.

In answering the question 'what business are we in?', here are some of the factors to consider:

- the customer needs which the business is trying to meet and the way those needs are changing for the future

- the point in the supply chain the business occupies – manufacturer, intermediary or retailer

- who exactly the business competes with as (a) core competition, and (b) as potential substitute products

- its geographical scope of operations

- the types of products or services it offers

- definition of organizational capability, now and in the future

- a realistic appraisal of its size and resources

- the organization's roots/history/founding purpose and track record

- the core skills/technology/market knowledge it possesses.

A business can be defined in a way that is product-oriented or customer-oriented. For example, a company could say 'we bend pipes', which is what it does, or it could say 'we provide lubrication transport solutions', which broadens the scope of how it thinks about itself and focuses on the buyer's need for a solution.

The answer to the question 'what business are we in?' takes the form of a mission statement, which should take account of the above key issues. This statement of the corporate mission provides, or should provide, a guiding vision for everyone in the organization. In fact, in developing mission statements, objectives and strategies, everyone working for the organization should be involved.

Of course, a manufacturer's context is largely defined by the production capability. The machinery installed in the facility defines what it can do, and therefore to a considerable extent what markets, games or businesses it's in or can enter. The more specialized the kit, the less flexibility the company has. Ford cannot use its car plant to make plastic buckets.

Companies can achieve flexibility by subcontracting or outsourcing their operations requirements. A lot of companies are saying: 'We don't need to make anything. Our subcontractor in Mexico, Hungary or China has the production capability and the economics are cheaper. We will just do the marketing, focus on the customer end and add value by designing the solution.' But there's a price to pay for this.

MARKETING MYOPIA

In a famous article way back in 1960, entitled 'Marketing myopia', Theodore Levitt reviewed the short-sightedness of certain industries, in particular the oil industry. By defining its business too narrowly, the oil industry failed to spot and defend itself adequately against significant threats posed by technological change. It was only its good fortune in stumbling across opportunities that prevented it being wiped out.

In determining the business the company is in, the definition must be wide enough to take in both the credible substitutes and the buyers' core needs and benefits. It is better to have a wide definition than a narrow one, as the risk of being outflanked is then smaller.

Defining the business the organization is in will shape its vision and focus. This means that some areas will therefore be excluded from the annual scanning of the business environment. It's vital that no significant relevant area or issue is left out. If you're not expecting it, you won't see it. If the vision isn't accurate, mistakes will be made.

BUSINESS-TO-BUSINESS MARKETS

Organizations that supply other businesses are in a different game from those that supply end-users or individual consumers. Business markets differ from consumer markets in a number of ways which have implications for marketing strategy and implementation:

● bigger customers with greater buying power, large annual spend, large volumes and more demanding requirements

● professional buying departments, well educated, organized, highly trained, with excellent market knowledge and strong technical and systems support

● a long distance from the final consumer – for example, the materials supplier providing sand for TV screen manufacture is a long way from the end consumer, the person who buys the TV set. The sand is sold first to the screen-maker, who sells to the tube-maker, then on to the set-maker and the retailer before reaching the consumer

- bigger sales contracts, more money at stake, a larger investment required to meet standards, and cut-throat competitor activity

- more complex sales and purchasing process giving longer order and payment lead times, with significant investment and cash flow implications

- involvement of a large number of people with a wide variety of requirements

- the presence of specifiers who don't do the buying, but effectively control what are the order-qualifying and order-winning criteria because they decide the specification of the product or service being sourced

- technically more complex products requiring greater technological inputs, continual innovation and technical improvement

- global sourcing, which means suppliers have to be prepared at a certain level to fight on a global battleground, if necessary developing the capability to become a sole supplier on a global basis.

BUSINESS-TO-BUSINESS BUYING
The amount of business transacted between companies, organizations and governments far exceeds the amount of business done between organizations and private consumers. The variety of business-to-business transactions is infinite. Here are some examples:

- Michelin supplies tyres to Renault

- a customer services management company handles the freephone service for a personal loans provider

- Arthur Andersen facilitates an off-site strategic planning workshop for a Fortune 500 corporation

- a sawmill provides timber components to a pallet maker

- a Macey's buyer attends the Paris ready-to-wear shows

- a food multiple sources chilled cabinets for its deli department

- Glaxo supplies drugs to a hospital

- a trade moulder supplies cabinetry to a computer vendor

- Boeing sources engines from Rolls-Royce

- a joinery company sells staircases to a housebuilder

- a textile plant supplies floorcovering for the Forte hotel chain

- a Ford dealer gets the contract to provide a fleet of trucks for the local engineering distributor

- Compaq sells its products direct to a bank

- a firm of executive search consultants headhunts a new chief executive for a publicly quoted corporation.

SIX KEY QUESTIONS

Once a company's board or group of executives or directors has decided what business it is in, there are six further questions related to that market which need to be worked out before the context can be described.

How big is the market?

In business markets this can be a surprisingly difficult question to answer. A lot of business people don't know the answer to this basic question, because they've never researched it. Others say the question isn't relevant, because their business is local, or they're just a small operator, or, better still, a niche operator, which is supposed to sound more 'cool'. There's no point, however, in being a trendy, cool operator, if you don't know the size of the niche.

Further business people say it's not meaningful to talk about market size when a company has only a 1 per cent share. Take, for example, the insurance market, where there are many players on 1 or 2 per cent. However, the important question is: what is this a percentage of? Everything is relative. To have 1 or 2 per cent of the insurance business is still to be a multi-million dollar business. So market size *is* important.

Fudging the question of market share often just means that businesses are too lazy to find out. It's an excuse for poor vision. If a company doesn't think the size of its market is important, then it must think market share isn't important, which is a risky point of view.

One way of calculating market size is to add up the output for the sector, add in imports and subtract exports, to give the size of the national market. Government statistics, however, are designed for economic management purposes, not to be helpful for salespeople or marketers. They're seldom sufficiently disaggregated to be of any help to anyone! In any case, the market may not in practice be broken down by geographical area or country – it may be continent-wide. So what is your organization's perspective? Does it define itself in local, regional, national, international, continental or global terms? Does it manufacture locally for a national market or globally for a global market?

Adding up the turnover of one's own company or division and the sales figures of the competitors is another way to work out market size. However, this can often be an unreliable guide. Product ranges don't match exactly, so you may sell products or services which one or more of your competitors don't provide. There may be differences in product definition, size, production process, technology and cost structure which could mean you are comparing apples with oranges. A third issue creating difficulties in assessing market size is that markets have submarkets or segments. Segmentation is discussed fully in chapter six, when we consider strategy. For now, it's enough to state that there can be different segments of a market, for example, geographic, size and type of application, which make market size calculation difficult. Also, the turnover of other players, even if publicly available, may include sales figures for non-relevant products. It's impossible to strip the irrelevant figures out without using covert intelligence! Finally, companies may be too small to need to disclose their financial position through the regulatory authorities to the public.

Why is market size such an important question? For one thing, size is often used by companies as an index of attractiveness of a market or segment. If it's a big, fast-growing market, offering lots of money-making potential and with no competitors in sight, then that will suggest a completely different set of investment, marketing and competitive decisions from those to be made if it's a small, zero-growth, 'everybody loses' dogfight!

How fast is the market growing? Speed of growth is a key feature of any market, but growth should always be seen in the context of market size. Growth rates of 40, 50, or even hundreds of per cent can be achieved in the early stages of a product's introduction, because you are working off a low base figure. In the later stages of a product's life, growth slows down and flattens off, providing a more competitive environment.

The concept of the market life cycle suggests that every product has a cycle of introduction, growth, maturity and decline. Total sales in the market of a particular service or category of product ramp up quickly in the introductory and growth stages with a flattening off at maturity and decline as demand or technology moves on. Profits lag behind the sales curve as the need to recover the cost of investment means a delay before these kick in, typically in the growth and maturity stages. The market life cycle concept can have considerable importance for competitive analysis, which is dealt with under the third C, competition, below.

There are other cyclical forces at work, for example, the economic cycle of recession and growth. Some industries have longer economic cycles than others, so it's important to get a view of the long-term trend. Some industries have a faster recovery rate and come out of recession ahead of others. Seasonality may also be an issue affecting the pattern of demand over the course of the trading year.

**TRICKS OF
THE TRADE**

○ *The market life cycle, economic cycle and seasonal factors need to be identified and, if possible, quantified or weighted in some way to help assess their importance and future impact.*

○ *Software-based sales forecasting and statistical techniques can be used for this purpose.*

How competitive is the market? The two simplest ways to measure competitiveness are market concentration and market share. Once market size has been determined, the different competitors' share can be worked out from their relevant product or service revenue. Expressing this revenue as a percentage of market size gives you the market share for each player, in value terms. Establishing the volume share is more tricky, but extremely useful. A company's value and volume shares may differ considerably. A niche operator that serves a small, highly specialized segment which pays big money for the right product may have a small volume share but a large value share of the overall market.

Markets with a high concentration ratio tend to be more competitive. If, for example, three organizations in a market account for 75 per cent of the sales, the market power is highly concentrated in their hands. In such a market, all sales will be fiercely contested by the big three.

How profitable is the market?

It's surprising how many companies don't always have a clear idea of how much profit they're making from the sales of some of their products and services. The issue can be complicated if a company has, for example, a range of 1,500 building products which it sells off a catalogue, quoting a list price for each one and offering cash discounts for bulk purchase or early payment to favoured customers.

If it's difficult to determine one's own product/service profitability, it's even more complex an exercise to identify accurately the total profit being taken out of a market in any period. Figures from speculatively undertaken market research reports, from competitors' annual reports or filed with the public authorities are a useful start but should be treated with caution, because almost always they are not broken down to a level where they can be helpful.

If the management or shareholders are not clear what level of profit is coming out of the market and which customers are driving that profit level, how can they make any judgement on their investment? It may be, and often is, the case that the shareholders would get a better return by putting their funds on deposit with a bank.

Where are the opportunities?

An opportunity is a set of circumstances favourable to the achievement of the company's objectives. If your organization is big enough, an opportunity can be internal – for example, an unmet need of a sister division.

There are two kinds of opportunities:

● opportunities for everybody

● opportunities for your company only.

For example, the introduction of the ISO9000 quality standard was an opportunity for everybody. Any company could apply for certification as an ISO9000 supplier. An opportunity which is unique to an individual company usually arises because of some special competitive advantage or product/service offering that company possesses, for example, a patent.

What are the threats?

Threats are those issues, developments or organizations external to the firm which may harm the firm in the achievement of its objectives. The primary and constant threat in any context, unless you are a fortunate monopolist, is always the competition, which is dealt with as the third C below.

There are many other sources of threats, such as the speed of change in technology. Some markets are less vulnerable to this, but the pace of technological change is increasing, and whole industries are being wiped out in a few years.

Some events can be opportunities as well as threats. For example, once the first company in any market had successfully adopted the ISO9000 quality standard it became a threat to everyone who had not yet been certified. Being first is critical, as an opportunity mastered by a competitor quickly becomes a threat.

WATCH OUT!

○ *Quite often, when people are asked to think about the opportunities for their organization, they come up with comments such as, 'Develop a new product' 'Enter the telecommunications market' or 'Diversify'. This equates opportunity with an action by the organization. Strictly speaking, this is not accurate. An opportunity is not an action, but a set of circumstances favourable to the achievement of the company's objectives.*

○ *From a business point of view, an opportunity is an* unmet buyer need, *which the company can fulfil better than or ahead of its competitors.*

○ *An unmet buyer need may be a need that the buyer is aware of but cannot solve. It can also be a need of which he or she isn't aware or only dimly aware and hasn't yet formulated or specified.*

○ *When analyzing the market for opportunities, look at the buyers' needs and see which ones could be met better. A significant aid in this process is the use of segmentation and targeting techniques which are described in chapter six.*

○ *Understand what business you're in.*

○ *Understand the nature of business-to-business markets.*

○ *Answer the six questions:*

1 *How big is the market?*

2 *How fast is the market growing?*

3 *How competitive is the market?*

4 *How profitable is the market?*

5 *Where are the opportunities?*

6 *What are the threats?*

TRICKS OF THE TRADE

One of the biggest mistakes a marketer can make is not to define his or her context carefully. Sure, every organization needs to understand what business it's in and have that communicated to all its people. However, as soon as you firm up on context, you become at least partially blinded to what's not in focus – it's human nature! For example, if an organization decides to take a specialist, narrow focus, rather than a broad, all-things-to-all focus, it runs the risk of being outflanked if the basis of specialization becomes inoperable, such as through technological change.

○ *The real secret – always to be kept in mind and systematically checked out at business planning time – is that each organization operates in different contexts simultaneously. It is therefore necessary when thinking about the business to be able to shift context and look at things from different points of view – the broad market perspective or that of the particular niche your company may occupy.*

○ *It's like looking at those pictures psychologists like to show which have ambivalent meaning or interpretation: is the figure a candlestick, or is it two heads meeting and touching? A different perception produces a different meaning.*

○ *This flexibility in thinking could mean the difference between survival and extinction!*

customers

This, the second of the five Cs, is the first in business importance! Customers or prospective customers (prospects) are actually the most important of the five Cs, but you cannot really talk about customers without the business context first being clearly defined.

CUSTOMERS OR BUYERS?

We prefer the word 'buyer' rather than 'customer', because it conveys succinctly the customer's function, which is quite simply to buy, and also because that's what business-to-business customers call themselves – buyers.

BUSINESS-TO-BUSINESS BUYING

There are several parallels between individual consumer buying behaviour and organizational behaviour, but it's the differences which are crucial. So we're going to spend some time talking about issues around organizational buying which it's important to capture and absorb. Then we'll discuss some more specific aspects.

BUYING

In this book we're talking about the purchase of products and services from one business to another. It's important to bear in mind that there are many other ways in which organizations 'buy' or procure resources. When we buy people's services, we call it 'recruitment'. If a company 'buys' a foreign country's package of incentives and business environment as a place to invest a manufacturing facility, we call that foreign direct investment. These are both situations when companies buy things in a wider sense.

THE BUYING DEPARTMENT

The focus of this book is on buying organizations rather than individual consumers. As products have become more complex and the nature of organizations has changed in response to technological and economic factors, the buying department, function or group has become more complex, too. Several people will become involved in a buying decision on a business-to-business service or product:

● the purchasing director or purchase agent will have laid down the policy on sourcing

- the buyer, senior buyer or lead buyer will have responsibility for actually negotiating the contract

- engineering or technical co-workers will usually have laid down a specification for the product to be acquired

- marketing will be represented in the buying function, particularly with retail buyers, either in the form of a person or a specification

- quality engineers have a say in vetting the supplier's process compliance with strict standards.

The collection of people who take part in work on the buying decision is known as the buying centre. The composition of the buying centre can be different in different companies, or within the same company for buying different products, or even at different stages in the buying process.

BUYING CRITERIA Owing to their different perspectives, the different members of the buying centre will have different criteria for the purchase. The purchasing director will be concerned about strategic aspects of relationships with suppliers and the contribution these make to the organization's profitability and direction. He or she will tend to get involved in buying negotiations only if there's a major contract at stake, either in terms of cost of purchase – for example, a major piece of equipment – or in terms of a long-term contract which has significant implications for end-product cost. His or her criteria are likely to be strategic fit and overall cost of the relationship.

The buyer will be concerned with getting the best-cost, best-quality deal that works for the company.

The engineering or technical people will be concerned with the quality of the technical solution, the performance requirements of the products, and the performance ultimately required by the final user or consumer.

Marketing's criteria will be about the effect of cost on the on-selling price, about variety, design, appearance, performance, reliability and benefits to the final consumer.

Quality personnel will be looking to assess the management, process and product quality of the supplier.

In addition there are other requirements. For example, the financial strength of a supplier is a critical factor. As companies place more reliance on suppliers, they need to be aware of the risk of liquidity or gearing problems putting those suppliers out of business, with consequent disruption to the supplies.

EXAMPLE

The real cost of financially weak suppliers

A buyer for a global furniture and furnishings retailer 'lost' one of her key suppliers, which collapsed suddenly due to financial problems. She had to spend much of the next four months replacing that supplier with another company, and it was a further 18 months before the new supplier was giving the same quality and breadth of service as its failed competitor. This was a major disruption to her procurement programme and the temporary stockout resulted in loss of profitability for the corporation. ○

THE BUYING PROCESS

Some marketers still believe that they're the initiators of the buying process. The marketer is seen as the active party communicating with passive buyers who are too stubborn and dumb to see the benefits of the products he or she is selling. In fact, reality is completely different. The buying process is driven by professional buyers who know what they're looking for and are proactive and effective in their efforts to get it.

The stages in the buying process are listed below (we've taken a production buy as an example, because of the importance of manufacturing buying within business-to-business dealings as a whole):

- sourcing need arises

- formulation of specification

- identification of suppliers

- buyer forwards inquiry package/request to quote/bid including quotation support documentation (QSD) or tender documents

- potential suppliers forward quotation with supporting information

- evaluation of competing suppliers

- invitation of lead bidder(s) to discuss further

- plant visit/quality assessment

- final technical/quality/price/delivery discussions

- production order placed/contract issued

- supply of product commences

- evaluation of performance.

This is just a simple outline of what happens. In practice, each company and industry will have its own practices. The process is discussed in detail in chapter three, The buying process.

THE BUYING DECISION APPROACH

Research by Michele Bunn of the State University of New York at Buffalo, published in the *Journal of Marketing* (January 1993, Vol. 57, pp. 38–56) suggests that there are six different kinds of buying decision approaches:

- casual

- routine low priority

- simple modified rebuy

- judgmental new task

- complex modified rebuy

- strategic new task.

These terms are discussed in more detail in chapter five 'Getting the strategy right'.

By categorizing the kind of approach your buyers or prospects are taking to the buy decision, you can understand the market more clearly and develop an appropriate and effective response.

BUYER'S RISK

Another factor affecting the buying process is the risk to the buyer if the deal goes sour or the project doesn't live up to specifications. The greater the monetary value of the contract or the critical nature of the component, the bigger the risk to the buyer. This will be reflected in the exactitude of the process and the scrutiny by the sourcing company in executing its evaluation.

BUYER-SELLER RELATIONSHIP

In business marketing, the buyer and seller contract their organizations to set up a working relationship, which can involve a wide range of contacts and areas of communications between employees of both organizations.

The 'sale' may not be made, therefore, entirely by the business development director, the marketing manager or technical sales executive, but, partly, perhaps even to a considerable extent, by the production supervisor, the quality assurance team, the line worker or anyone else perceived by the buyer to be making a significant contribution. This aspect will be considered in more detail in chapter three.

BUYER INFORMATION

We have seen that when 'taking the market apart' to look at your customers, you need to understand the following general issues about buyers:

- departmental organization
- buying criteria
- buying process
- buying decision approach
- risk to buyer
- relationships.

In order to get the buyer information right there are also specific questions to be asked:

- How many prospects/buyers are there?
- Where are they located?
- What are their needs?
- How are they performing in terms of sales, profitability and winning new business for the future?
- If you're doing business with a particular company already, is the relationship working for you in terms of sales or profits success?
- What is the buyer's customer focus?
- Can buyers be grouped into categories which have similar characteristics?

- What are the order-qualifying and order-winning criteria?

- What are the buyers' plans for the future?

- Do they know about us? Do they know our name, reputation, capability, skills, products, services, concepts, successes, failures and plans for the future?

- Are we big enough, smart enough, flexible enough or skilled enough to cope comfortably with the requirements they will place on us?

ANALYZING BUYERS How do you analyze buyers? Very simple, if you know them, contact them and consult them.

You can run a buyer lead analysis by asking a series of questions. Did you get to know the buyers through a chance meeting in a plane, at a trade fair, or in response to an ad? Your top 5 or 10 accounts in the past 2 to 3 years – where have they come from? Were they the result of a specific trawl or accident?

How long does it take to book a customer's first order?

Examine the sales records. Which accounts are the most profitable and the most revenue-generating? Is there any distinct feature which groups the top 20 per cent? You could map them onto a grid like Figure 1.1 opposite. Then you have a management plan worked out for each of these segments. You need high profit, high volume accounts as they are the cream. Low volume, high margin accounts are still excellent but may need increasing. Low margin, high volume accounts are useful as a base load, but there's a risk if a major contract is lost. Low volume, low margin accounts need a good reason to be kept. If you cannot think of one, don't.

Figure 1.1

Buyer account analysis matrix

		SALES VOLUME	
		High	*Low*
PROFIT	*High*	Keep these buyers!	Seek to grow the sales volume.
	Low	Useful as capacity loading, but are you being used? Are you too dependent?	Meet, with a view to delisting.

DON'T FORGET!

○ *The general issues that arise when dealing with business-to-business buyers, rather than individual customers*

○ *The specific information that relates to your prospects or customers in the particular business context in which your company is operating.*

competitors

The simplest way of looking at competition is to say that your competitors are those businesses which are selling or trying to sell into the same account as your organization. So whether it's a competitor you are trying to displace from or keep out of an existing buyer account, it's extremely easy to identify to identify these players.

CORE COMPETITORS

There are some companies or organizations which are selling to precisely the same buyers as your company. You're in direct competition with them. They're your core competitors. Other companies present an indirect threat, but don't appear to be in the same market to the same extent. These are the non-core competitors. Clearly, the core competitors are the ones to watch out for. But be careful! Competition has many different dimensions and many hidden dangers.

WATCH OUT!

○ *Somewhere, unknown to you, a new process or product may be being developed which may not appear to be in the same business context as you define it, but in fact meets the same buyer need, in a new way. It's in effect a substitute product. If someone invents a filmless camera and you're in the film business, this could be the beginning of the end!*

○ *Your competitors may be planning a powerplay, i.e. a big move designed to radically alter the power relationships in the competitive game. For example, two core competitors may merge. Their combined salesforce and distribution coverage, combined with some judicious product rationalisation or new product development, will produce one major new competitive force.*

○ *A large corporation, which currently has no presence in your market, may decide that the prospects are good and set up a greenfield operation – a new manufacturing facility, the latest machines, optimized production process and layout, and some fresh recruits trained in innovative techniques and without the baggage of outdated work practices. This may take a year or more to happen, so there's time to react, but the scope and nature of the change is so great that any reaction needs to produce an effective counterweight, an initiative with an equally or more radical impact to rebalance the power factor.*

○ *A large company which has a subsidiary division operating in the same market as your company may decide to make a significant investment.*

○ *A new entrant may come in by way of acquisition, buy up an existing operator, acquiring the buyer base, the products, the process and the brand. They can then either go for an immediate investment or lie low till they work out which levers to pull to make the business work profitably and generate cash for them.*

HIDDEN COMPETITORS

Competition in the broader sense isn't just the people in your business trying to take buyers away from you. Other people are trying to take margin away from you as well: the buyers who take your product, the suppliers who provide you with your inputs, the makers of substitute products and new entrants lining up to take a crack at your market either with a new facility or by taking over and revitalizing a competitor.

COMPETING WITH BUYERS FOR MARGIN

There's always a risk that your buyers' company can decide to take the work you do in-house. Behind every purchasing decision, there's a 'make or buy' calculation – the purchasing company has worked out that, all things considered, it's better to buy in certain inputs than make them itself. That calculation can always change if the costs of the factors of production change. Or, if the volume of, say, a subassembler's work reaches a certain level, and the purchaser believes it could acquire the skills to make the subassembly, it may simply do the work itself. Although the risk of this may seem slight in view of the fact that many original equipment manufacturers are rationalizing their supply bases and farming more work out to the suppliers the risk, depending on the specific business context, may be much greater. Much will depend on the buying firm's organizational development policy and manufacturing strategy.

The principal way in which business-to-business salespeople/marketers are competing with their buyers, however, is that each is competing against the other for a share of the price to the end-buyer or final user and, therefore, each is competing with the other for margin.

The subassembler will always be looking to cut the cost of supply while maintaining or increasing its own price to the end-buyer. If it can succeed in this, it will widen its share of the stake and become more powerful.

COMPETING WITH SUPPLIERS FOR MARGIN

In a similar way, every company competes with its suppliers. They may decide that they want to get closer to the end-user and come looking to buy a company at your stage in the chain – for example buy a distributor, or buy your company or your core competitor. Also, they'll be looking for opportunities to increase prices either to pass on upward pressure on their own costs or simply to take more profit out of the value chain. If you grant an increase and cannot yourself recover it from the sale of your own products, you have lost margin from the chain.

Small companies buying materials from powerful suppliers for processing and onward sale to powerful buyers are particularly open to the risk of being squeezed in the middle, leading to severe margin compression, cash-flow difficulties and consequent lack of funds for innovation and expansion.

COMPETITION AND POWER

Despite all the talk of partnership sourcing and trust, the relationships between companies and their buyers and suppliers are based fundamentally on economic power.

Supplier power

Suppliers have power when the purchaser doesn't represent a big account to them and is therefore not a high priority. The fewer reliable or credible sources there are for the specific inputs you need, the more power suppliers have. The more of your spend that goes on the materials or components provided by the supplier company, the more critical is the relationship, the more dependent your company is, and the more leverage the supplier has over you. If it has proprietary technology or sole access to a natural resource or unique process, its power is immeasurably increased. Also, if your buyer tells you which supplier to use for a particular component, this increases the supplier's power considerably. You are being told: 'If you want to work with us, you've got to use so-and-so.'

Buyer power

Buyer power is exercised when your customer takes a significant percentage of your production, say over 30 per cent. This carries a major risk, because the buyer can find a better price elsewhere, then pull the plug on you, leaving you with overcapacity and a need to seek new accounts fast. If what you supply is non-critical and can be procured from 50 other suppliers, the buyer can switch easily.

LEADERS, CHALLENGERS, FOLLOWERS AND NICHERS

It's helpful when trying to analyze the competition to examine its share of the market compared to the other players. Research has shown that there are four main kinds of competitor in any market context:

- leader
- challenger
- follower
- nicher.

Leader, as the name implies, means the organization with the largest share of the market in value or volume terms. Being the leader is associated with certain types of behaviour, such as being first into the market with new products, or taking a lead on price reductions or increases. Watching the leader, if your own organization isn't in that fortunate position, is a very useful way to set a benchmark for your own performance.

A challenger means a company which is quite close to the leader in terms of market share and in a position to make a credible challenge to become the leader. Such a company often behaves aggressively in terms of pricing and promotion.

A follower is a company which is a good bit off the leadership position and unlikely to mount a successful challenge. The behaviour of followers is largely determined by what the leader does. They're not big enough, and don't have enough leverage, to really work to win. They tend to produce me-too products priced above those of the leader's and compete on non-price issues, such as delivery, service and design. They'll never have the resources to make an effective challenge for leadership. Low-share business operations like this can manage to make a living by staying flexible and developing lower-cost solutions.

A nicher is a specialist working in a small segment which requires highly specialized servicing and where the volumes are too small to attract the leader.

There is a fifth category of competitor, which isn't one that's likely to cause concern: losers. These are companies that are going out of business, slowly but surely. They limp along from year to year with a declining sales curve. The market trend is away from them, and most industries have them. There's no need to worry about them, unless you're unlucky enough to be working for them!

FAST TRACK

In studying your competitors you need to take a view on their objectives – are they going for share, or profitability? Sometimes this can be taken from a chairman's statement, or from trade information or industry information. Then you need to take a view on their strategy, in other words how they plan to achieve those objectives. Deductions about their objectives and strategies can be made from their behaviour – what they do and what they say about themselves.

INDUSTRY CONCENTRATION

A way of measuring the underlying intensity of competition in the market is to analyze the sales turnover of the top three or five companies. If their combined turnover reaches more than 50 per cent, the market can be said to be concentrated, depending on the number of other competitors. This figure is known as the concentration ratio. The higher the ratio, i.e. the greater the degree of concentration in the market, the tougher the competition will be.

THE BASIS OF COMPETITION

Any aspect of operations can become a basis for successful competition, provided always that it's meaningful to the buyer and reflects some kind of distinctive competence. The scale of operations can be a basis of competition, as can engineering skill, branding, patents/proprietary technology and coverage of the market.

A bigger product range can be a very effective basis for competition. A competitor could have a bigger product range, which could get it through more doors.

EXAMPLE

An interior design consultant usually carries brochures on furnishings, colour schemes and lighting. If targeting the office market, he or she could also carry brochures for office furniture. This enables him or her to offer a package to architects or facilities managers who like to minimize the sources they use. The design consultant can quote for the design, furnishing, decoration and furniture. This extra capability is a competition-beater as far as some clients are concerned.○

COMPETITOR APPRAISAL

In chapter six, we introduce the concept of the buyer relationship framework for handling buyers. A more detailed explanation can be found there. Apart from serving as a useful guide to the management of relationships with buyers, it can also be used for comparing your own company's strengths and weaknesses with those of key rivals.

Table 1.1 shows a list of the seven elements in the buyer relationship framework, together with a short-list of issues to consider as a basis of comparison with the competition. In addition, the competitors' financial strengths or weaknesses should be taken into account, including sales, profit and share price trends.

Table 1.1

Competitor evaluation using buyer relationship management mix	
Buyer relationship framework	*Issues to consider*
Buyer management	Key buyer accounts analysis Accounts or bids won and lost Market share and share growth check Resource allocation
Buyer need	Range of products and services Innovative capability Time to market
Buyer cost	Pricing objectives Pricing strategies Cost base
Buyer information and communications	Management of communications media Message content Positioning statement
Buyer convenience	Logistics management Delivery performance/JIT capability Plant locations
Bought quality	Quality statement Quality drivers used Quality awards held
Bought process	Operational process used Machinery and equipment capability Scale of output

COMPETITORS' PRODUCTS

When looking at competitors, it's vital to be thorough. One of the most practical and productive actions to take is to buy their products and take them apart. It's what the Japanese have so often done! A small but revealing test of the company's seriousness about acquiring competitor intelligence is whether a budget can be released to acquire competing products, and executive and engineering time allocated to studying them.

A view should be formed on competitors' speed of reaction.

○   *Will they react quickly?*

○   *In what area are you weakest?*

○   *Can they hit you there?*

○   *Where can they attack you?*

COMPETITION – IT'S A GAME OF TWO HALVES

When a top football team plays an important game, it prepares thoroughly. This usually involves watching a video of the opponents. While this is useful, it's only a half-measure. It misses out a completely different crucial dimension.

The key to really understanding your opponent or competition is to be able to *put yourself in its position*, knowing its strengths and weaknesses, and imagine how you would play against you if you were in that situation! It means looking at your team through unaccustomed eyes, having the mental skill or dexterity to flip out of one mode of thinking and slip into a strange or foreign way of thinking. It means taking a cold look from the opposite side at how strong your team really is. Is your star player really that good, or will the opposite number mark him or her out of the game? Can your pattern of play be disrupted? Where do you seem comfortable, fat or exposed? What are the weak points? What strategy would you use to disrupt your own team's performance? What unsettles your team? What makes your players start criticizing each other? When do they begin to get frustrated? How would you as the opposition create the conditions to bring these things about?

So you aren't just trying to beat the opposing team at the game of football, or even at *your* game of football, but also at *their* game of football. The competitor will see and read the structure and flow of the game differently, and unless you take account of this different way of thinking about the game, you are not playing in the same ball game, even though you are on the same football field.

Another sporting analogy about competition stems from the athletics track. There's no point running the 1500m as if it was just you against the clock, the wind and the track surface. You have to take account of your competitors' moves and styles of running. If your key competitor has a powerful kick off the last bend and a fast finish, you might try to tire him or her out before the last lap. But that would only make sense if it suited your own racing skills. There's no point in trying to change your whole style just to deal with the competition. You've got to work with your own strengths.

DON'T FORGET!

○ *In addition to direct or core competitors, a company is also competing for margin with those who buy from it and act as suppliers to it for a stake in the margin available in the value chain.*

○ *Competitors should be thoroughly analyzed using a suitable framework, either the critical success factors (see below) or the buyer relationship framework (see chapter six).*

critical success factors (CSFs)

A critical success factor is any factor which is critical to the success of the business. They are, in fact, the secrets of success in your operating context. This applies at two levels. Firstly, in the specific business context, for example, the airline business, and, secondly, at company level, where there are certain factors you need to get right in a particular business situation.

For the purposes of this discussion, context means the industry and its dynamics, and situation means what's going on at any given time, for example, whether the company is planning to launch a new product. Each business context and each business situation has different critical success factors.

How can a business development executive know what are the critical factors for the business? Well, essentially, by taking the market apart as we've done in this chapter so far. Firstly define the context, secondly study the customers and thirdly analyze what the competition is doing. The output from these processes will give a clear indication of what is critical for success in the present context and situation.

Another way to identify them is to take a good look at the market leader (within your definition of the market context) and see how your organization differs from it. Those areas of difference are the difference between leadership and non-leadership.

Critical success factors can be either a corporate capability (ability to grow quickly, ability to cut costs dramatically) or relate to a specific function (hiring the right front-line staff in a service business, using a quality ad agency, process engineering, or research and development).

How many CSFs are there? It depends entirely on the context and situation. If a marketing manager conducts analysis and uncovers, say, 15 factors which he or she believes to be critical for success, this isn't helpful. A useful rule of thumb is that there should be no more than five. This is because the benefit of identifying them is to provide a focus for the organization. Any more than five important things to think about and organizations can become confused, lacking in focus.

At the same time, having just one CSF provides an extremely clear focus, and single-minded pursuit of this factor for success may be all a company needs. However, such a narrow focus may not do justice to the complexity of the context in which the organization operates. For example, a manufacturing facility may focus on one single factor, production yield, but fail to get its delivery scheduling right, thereby upsetting its customers. In the long run, a balanced set of factors is wiser.

As well as providing a focus, equally importantly CSFs can be expressed quantitatively and performance benchmarked against them. For example, taking the market apart may suggest that a load factor of 90 per cent is critical for the success of a jet cargo operation. This can easily be tracked and measured from week to week. Also timely delivery, defined as within half an hour either side of a given time, can be tracked and measured from records as a percentage of total deliveries.

It's important to understand not only the critical success factors for your own product-market, but also those of your buyers in their markets. Often the buyers' critical success factors will translate into those factors or criteria which they present to you as requirements.

A quick way of coming to the crux of critical success factors is to look at the order-qualifying and order-winning criteria for your business. Order-qualifying criteria are those which the product or service offering has to match simply to be able to compete or even asked to quote. Order-winning criteria are those aspects of the buyer's concerns which make the difference between getting the business or being second.

Order-winning criteria aren't always the whole story. They're a subset of critical success factors, or a useful shorthand for describing them. The CSF analysis takes into account the building blocks which need to be carefully constructed, the launch pad which the organization needs before it can qualify. In Table 1.2 below are some examples of critical success factors

Table 1.2

Examples of critical sucess factors	
Business	*Success factor*
Airline	Load factor Safety record
Plant hire	Availability
Automotive component manufacture	Ford QSS rating or equivalent Timely delivery
Holding company	Skill at acquisition, management and disposal of operating units
Property construction	Site acquisition/land bank
International business relocation	Serviced site availability Attractive incentive package
DIY products	Listing with retail multiples
PC screen manufacture	Production yield
Pharmaceuticals	Size and quality of R&D operation

CSFs AND COMPETITION

The nature of CSFs can be determined as much by the power and basis of competition as by the structural elements of the industry. Each competitor shapes the market through its behaviour.

DON'T FORGET!

Critical success factors are those factors which can make or break your organization. They depend on:

○ *the nature of the business context and situation*

○ *the needs of specific prospects or buyers*

○ *the power of the competition*

○ *the strengths and weaknesses of your organization.*

company

The next aspect of the market to take apart is the fifth C, the company, i.e. the organization, firm, hospital, agency or conglomerate for which you work.

WHICH COMPANY ARE WE TALKING ABOUT?

It's important to be clear about what operating unit is being examined. Ideally it's an organization focused on a particular type of buyer. It's important also that the buyer focus targets are clearly worked out, otherwise there may be confusion between marketing strategy and corporate strategy.

MISSION, OBJECTIVES AND STRATEGY

When taking your own company apart, you need to be clear about the following:

● the mission

● the corporate objectives, for example, return on investment percentage

● corporate strategy, for example, growth by acquisition

● the marketing objectives, for example, increased market share

- marketing strategy, for example, new market development

- competitive objectives, for example, the displacement of a major competitor from a key account

- the competitive strategy, i.e. who the company is targeting and how, for example, cost leadership, differentiation or specialization.

All of these key components are discussed in greater detail in chapter five.

COMPANY APPRAISAL

An appraisal of your company should be carried out in order to assess its marketing performance, strengths and weaknesses. You should look at the following factors.

Objectives

What is the corporate objective for return on investment?

Buyer segmentation

Has the company segmented the buyers/prospects? Has it broken the demand down into manageable chunks which can be intuitively grasped as having distinct needs? On what basis has it done so: industry application, size, location, buying situation?

Buyer targeting

Has the company gone after everyone indiscriminately? Has it focused on a few key segments to target? Which are they? On what basis has the targeting been done?

The key criteria for target segment selection are:

- potential profitability

- size

- growth trend

- distinct customer needs

- critical success factors

- intensity of competition

- the company's distinctive offering.

If the company has been targeting segments, is the basis of targeting still valid? Is the company targeting a wide range of segments with a range of distinct offerings, or is it focused narrowly, specializing in serving one small group of customers?

Given the range of distinct groups of customers being targeted, whether wide or narrow, what is the company's competitive positioning within those segments? This is drawn from a careful consideration of the segment customers' needs and the sustainable competitive advantage which the company enjoys. It is essentially a statement of what customers the company is targeting and how it will compete. The latter point includes how it will position its products or services in the prospects' and customers' minds. (See pages 170–71 for further discussion.)

Product/service evaluation

A detailed value analysis of the product or service can be carried out. There should be a systematic analysis of the product in the light of competitors' offerings, and of the features and the benefits it delivers in the light of properly researched buyer needs.

Price

Apart from analyzing the company's pricing compared to competitors, there should be a complete review of the company's cost base and its effect on price. Factors which add unnecessarily to cost should be identified. Ways of changing the operational process and product design should be considered in order to lower cost without negatively affecting quality.

Communications

All aspects of the company's communications should be examined. These break down into five broad areas:

- internal communications
- buyer communications, both existing and potential
- supplier communications
- shareholder communications
- community communications.

You should ask the following questions:

- What are the communications objectives?

- What communications media are used?

- What messages are communicated?

- Who are the communications targets?

Distribution/ supply chain management/ logistics

The following questions should be considered on the subject of supplies and product distribution management:

- Are your logistics in line with expectations?

- How do logistics fit with operations management?

- Is the logistics strategy harmonized with the product positioning?

- Are contract operators used?

- Is information tightly controlled?

- Are service levels regularly checked and worked out?

- Are transaction costs minimized?

- Is electronic data interchange (EDI) in use?

- Is a 'just-in-time' (JIT) or similar system in operation, inbound and outbound?

- Is there a buyer satisfaction index in place, including specific measures of excellence in terms of timeliness, accuracy and flexibility of delivery?

- Is the logistics function evaluated on a return on assets basis as well as a cost basis?

Marketing assets

What are the key assets that the company has in marketing terms? Obviously, a well-known brand is a marketing asset, although branding is under-utilized in business-to-business markets. Other examples would include superior products, wide distribution coverage, a responsive logistics capability, a well-trained and highly motivated salesforce, patents, a global supply capability, manufacturing flexibility and fast time-to-market for new services or products.

Since the critical success factors are so vital to success or failure in the market, they form an extremely useful basis of comparison when you evaluate the company's strengths and weaknesses against those of the core competitors. To do this you should:

● identify the CSFs

● weight the CSFs out of 100

● score the company and its competitors out of 10 against each of the CSFs

● total the scores for the company and competitors

● draw the necessary conclusions about the company's standard of excellence, or otherwise!

An example of this process is provided in Table 1.3 opposite. Clearly, this method has some sensitivities. The weights for the critical success factors and the scores out of 10 are subjective. The partial antidotes to this are:

● try to make sure that the CSF weighting and company marks are based on as much hard data as possible

● get a group of colleagues to participate in the exercise and discuss the validity of the weights and scores with reference to actual events and hard data.

Table 1.3

Comparison of company and competitors against critical success factors (CSFs)
Tube manipulation business

Critical success factor (CSF)	Weighting (Percentage)	Company (Mark/10)		Competitor A (Mark/10)		Competitor B (Mark/10)		Competitor C (Mark/10)	
		Mark/10	Score	Mark/10	Score	Mark/10	Score	Mark/10	Score
Flexible production	0.45	8	3.6	6	2.7	6	2.7	8	3.6
Product development capability	0.35	6	2.1	6	2.1	4	1.4	8	2.8
JIT delivery	0.20	9	1.8	7	1.4	4	0.8	9	1.8
TOTALS	1.00		7.5		6.2		4.9		8.2

The three critical success factors have been identified as flexible production, product development capability and JIT delivery. These have been weighted as 0.45, 0.35 and 0.2 respectively. The company has a weighted score of 7.5, which is good, but not the best. Competitor C has a score of 8.2, because of its superior product development capability. This is a company weakness on this critical factor and needs to be remedied.

Once the strengths and weaknesses of the company have been assessed against the CSFs in this way, the findings can be pulled together in a SWOT analysis (an appraisal of the company's strengths, weaknesses, opportunities and threats). This is dealt with in more detail in chapter five, 'Getting the strategy right'.

Every other function or process should be carefully examined for strengths and weaknesses: finance and accounting, human resources, quality, supply chain management and operations.

FAST TRACK

marketing research

The activity of information gathering is called marketing research (MR). This is how you can spot opportunity. Some people who've had experience of marketing research feel it can be too bound up in codes of conduct to be effective. That will be discussed later on, when we take a look at agency research. In fact, the kind of MR we have in mind is more focused on prospecting and hard, relevant market information.

WHAT HAPPENS IF YOU DON'T DO ANY MARKETING RESEARCH?

- At least some of your competitors will and they'll inevitably get a competitive advantage in intelligence.

- You won't know where you're going, and if you don't know that, your objectives and strategy will be weakened.

- You won't know where the opportunities are coming from or who's best positioned to take advantage of them.

- You won't be as effective in influencing the buying decision as you could be.

- You won't know how big the market is, what the underlying forces of competition are, how the market is changing or how it breaks down into market share.

- You won't know what your competitors are doing or scheming to do.

- To get feedback as an everyday activity.

- It can give you a map of the market, showing who sells what to whom in what quantities and at what prices.

- It can assess buyer attitudes and predict their behaviour.

- It can provide a careful insight into the kind of criteria trade-offs that buyers make, in terms of price, quality, timely delivery, product or service attributes.

- It can assess the effectiveness of distribution strategy.

- It can help predict technological changes in the product.

- It can be used in acquisitions.

- It can identify customer opportunities.

- In international marketing it can be used to profile different countries as entry targets and also to analyze modes of entry, whether simple exports or full manufacturing presence.

- It can warn of environmental threats.

- It can check the effectiveness of the organization's communications.

- It can assess the strengths and weaknesses of the company's buyer handling.

In short, MR can focus usefully on almost any aspect of business and provide critical nuggets of information.

WATCH OUT!

○ *There are costs and risks in conducting MR and they apply to every business activity. The answer to the risks and costs lies in the management of values and priorities.*

○ *If a company values a constant flow of accurate information about its business activities and the competitor and customers, and if it believes in the need for effective decision-making and in the quality of its own thinking, it will value marketing research.*

To take the market apart, it's necessary to be familiar with sources of information. Use of data should start with internal data, which is readily available and inexpensive to extract. Then, external sources of data should be accessed, starting with secondary data, such as government reports and statistics, annual reports of competitors, and buyers' organizations, stock exchange prospectuses, analysts' reports and speculative market research reports.

Most of this data is available quite inexpensively. If, however, someone wants primary data, that is to say data which is specially procured or custom-sourced, for an organization's needs, that is going to cost more than a few hundred dollars.

It's at this stage that you encounter the second roadblock on the highway to understanding the market, namely, companies' unwillingness to invest in marketing research. (The first roadblock is the – unfounded and absurd! – fear of paralysis by analysis.)

Marketing research is often dismissed by 'practical' executives who 'know how this business works'. In reality, they are secretly too mean to invest the money! Often, executives who express this attitude are technical people who see every 'extra' as an on-cost and begrudge the money unless it's going into the purchase of a machine. This book, however, strongly advocates the use of systematic and regular marketing research. It also encourages an investment view of MR rather than a cost view.

**DRIVING WHILE
BLIND**

Imagine you join a multi-lane freeway at speed, get into the middle lane and close your eyes! Your hands are still on the steering wheel, but you aren't in control of the situation. Sure, you know where the gas pedal and brake are, but after a short while you'll have absolutely no idea where you're going and become a danger to yourself and others. Well, that's like running a business or a sales/marketing process without marketing research.

Marketing research is the eyes of the business. Without eyes, you can't see and your information inflow is radically restricted. This has to affect the quality of your thinking. There's no way you can be as smart or switched on as your competitors or buyers if you're blind or half-blind to what is going on in the market.

Like training, advertising and even research and development, marketing research is usually a candidate for the axe when times are tough. If you work in a company run by engineers (often run for the engineers, not for the buyers), defending marketing research against cuts is often a losing battle. Engineers, technical people and production people are into how things work. They excel, once they've gotten the contract, at delivering the goods. If they've got work, if there's enough work to keep them going for another six to twelve months, they're not going to worry too much about where the next contract comes from.

Accountants are driven by return on investment and cost reduction. That's fine. Every business should own that focus. But accountants are trained to be prudent and cautious, to be risk-averse and not to spend on activities that seem to cost more than the benefits they provide. Marketing research can often be regarded by this kind of mindset as a waste of money. Yet there's far more to business than cost control and return on investment. Above all, business is about opportunity, which is about buyers and that is where sales and marketing come in!

OPPORTUNITY   Let's face it, many people are hired because they can be trusted to do what they're told. They're reliable, productive, can cope, react quickly to a crisis and keep things under control – above all, they can manage. Well, that's fine, but for opportunity search you need a different mindset, a genuine business mindset. This is what used to be called business acumen, but has now been appropriated by accountants!

Opportunity search is a subtle art. There are so many things that can get in the way, so many obstacles blocking the route. Fear of failure and fear of risk are two of the biggest.

Opportune was originally a term applied to the wind. For sailors it meant a wind which drove the ship towards the port of destination. So an opportunity is something that takes you where you need or want to go, something which helps you achieve your overall objective, reach your goal. The word 'opportunity' also contains the sense of possibility or likelihood. In strategic management jargon, people often talk about an opportunity gap or window or a strategic window, a space into or through which the company can move to set up a better position. More concretely, an opportunity could be an invitation to tender for a construction contract, a request for quotation or the failure of a competitor and therefore a gap in the market.

If the engineers are focused on the machinery, the cabling and the technology and the accountants are focused on the cash-flow, bank relationship, profitability, cost control and return on investment, who's looking after the buyer? What opportunities exist for recruiting new buyers? What opportunities exist for retaining existing buyers?

There's a truth about management, which has to do with 'management by default'. When someone buys a new software package, it usually comes with default settings. Unless you make a conscious effort to change those default settings, the computer will always work to them. If you want to make the PC work to your requirements, the default settings have to be called up in the dialog box and suitably altered.

It's the same with management. Life goes on, and the business trundles along. People get up in the morning and come to work. They have a job and some idea of where they're going. So as long as they keep getting paid, that's OK. Underlying all of this day-to-day activity are the settings which channel the work effort and energies of the company's workers. Those settings need to be looked at regularly to check that they're appropriate.

A strategy is all about how something is done. The company's marketing research strategy is about how the company handles MR. That may be the result of a conscious policy or conscious decision-making, or it may simply be a drift – the default strategy, the unconscious settings.

The rule of default says that if you don't have a conscious strategy, you have a default strategy. A default strategy is a mish-mash of assumptions, one-off reactions, confusion and fuzzy objectives. It's not focused and it doesn't know where it's going. In other words, if MR isn't thought through carefully and accurately, the company will get the MR it deserves – ineffective and risky.

If the company hasn't the skill, experience or time to conduct the inquiry it decides it needs, it can hire an agency to do the work.

Hiring an MR agency

An MR agency can provide an independent, objective, third-party view, which is often a useful point of reference and leverage in winning arguments about priorities and work programmes. The agency can also provide anonymity, screening your company from the competition while it makes enquiries.

The same criteria apply to hiring an MR agency/consultancy as to hiring any other agency – advertising, media relations, or exhibition design. They are:

- track record

- cost.

Track record means experience in the product or service market in which the company operates. This should have given the agency experience in working with a list of players in the business and contacts in a few key ones. The agency's client list will offer evidence of this.

Cost is a function of day rate and methodology. The day rate is often better, i.e. cheaper, in a regional rather than a national agency. Methodology depends entirely on the question that's being asked.

Commissioning research puts you in the role of buyer, about which we have a lot to say elsewhere in this book!

Formulating the question

The first thing to do is to understand the nature of the question that requires resolving. Think about the issue. Kick it around with a few colleagues, not just from marketing, sales or business development, but from finance and operations as well. If it's a business problem, it needs a holistic perspective. It may even be possible to discuss the issue with a buyer that you know and trust. This would give an excellent perspective.

Identifying agencies

The next step is to locate a directory of MR agencies. These directories are usually produced by MR associations on behalf of their agency members. The agencies are listed by specialization, e.g. electronics or telecommunications, and by the type of work they do, e.g. quantitative studies, focus groups, etc.. Using the index, it's possible to short-list five or six agencies that do work relevant to your company's context.

Call them with a rough idea of what you're looking for. The purpose of the call isn't to get into an in-depth discussion of methodologies or issues, it's simply to get the shortlist down to the three that appear to speak your language, can talk sensibly and accurately about what's going on in your market in general and maybe can mention a couple of names of people or companies that indicate they know what they're talking about. Ask them to send any prospectus or company information they have.

Briefing

The next step is to invite three of them to your office to take a briefing, as you'll need a few quotes. Even if one of them stands out, still get three quotes. The essential point is this: it's in the comparison that the pros and cons of the right agency come into focus.

The beauty of briefing MR agencies, indeed any agencies, is that it's a fantastic learning opportunity. In one day, with three 2–3 hour meetings, you can learn a lot, mostly about your own company!

The agencies, in order to take a good brief, have to ask questions. The more questions they ask, the more you have to think, and the more perspectives are opened up on the research question. Gradually, inevitably, the 'killer issues' emerge clearly into focus.

The better the agency, the better the questions it will ask. Remember, its whole business is about asking questions and getting answers. At the end of each meeting, do you have the impression of having being courteously, but effectively and thoroughly, questioned? If you do, then the chances are that the agency's targets and respondents will too!

You too should ask questions. Does the agency understand your product, including any technical aspects, if the assignment is of a technical nature? What additional information does it need to ask relevant questions? Who do the agency's researchers know in the business? If they don't know many people in your business, are they going to have a lengthy learning curve? Are they acquiring new sectoral experience at your expense? What companies have they worked for before? Are those companies competitors? How recent is the work? Do they have any preferences or convictions about the best way of accessing the information or the best methodology? Will they be using freelance or subcontract operators? If so, what will be their role and briefing? How will they be quality-controlled? Bear in mind that at some point in the future, if the freelancer is a specialist in your area, it may be possible to hire him or her direct – although that'll need to be finessed carefully, as far as the agency is concerned!

Proposal Submission

The agencies will submit their fully costed proposals. You're then in a position to do what buyers do and compare and contrast the different offers. Inevitably, there'll be differences in methodology and daily rate. The selection decision is primarily about what methodology will get you the best answer to the key questions. At this stage cost is secondary, unless it's way out of line.

You also have the opportunity to pick and mix. In other words you can maybe decide to change the brief to take account of some new ideas that have come up from this work. Then call the leading contender and invite it in to work further on developing and fine-tuning its proposal to reflect the best of the thinking about research work on the key question.

Methodology

Methodology is a fancy word for strategy, which is a fancy word for how things are done. Marketing research methodology is a fancy phrase for how business information is collected. Here are the main methods:

- *Desk research* – use of published sources, such as directories, market reports and on-line databases

- *Personal interview* – a structured or loosely structured discussion with a respondent

- *Observation* – on-the-spot examination of what actually happens in a particular business operating context

- *Focus group* – a group discussion by informed and relevant respondents of a specific issue

- *Telephone interview* – usually talking a respondent through a questionnaire-type script

- *Mail survey* – a questionnaire mailed to targets.

In practice, much business-to-business marketing research will make use of desk research, telephone interview and personal interview.

Desk research should always be done first. Although the data thrown up by this process hasn't been originally generated to cater for the company's specific needs, it's cheap! It also provides a wider framework, can help to put the market situation in context and set up the really important and interesting questions for further exploration and discussion.

Another useful distinction in MR is between quantitative and qualitative data. Quantitative data are market size, shares, growth etc., i.e. anything to do with figures. Qualitative data are to do with insights, e.g. buyers' attitudes to new products or services, perceptions of suppliers and decision criteria.

There's much debate about the pros and cons of these types of data. It's easy to get lost in the technicalities in this area, but this distracts attention from the objective of inquiry, which is to get accurate, relevant, reliable and insightful information as inexpensively as possible.

FUNDING MARKETING RESEARCH

Of course, there's a potential downside to MR. It costs time, money and energy that could be spent on other things, like selling or promotion. There's also the risk that in conducting the research you inadvertently disclose to your competitors what you're doing. Business-to-business markets are quite often like small clubs, and word gets around about who's doing what.

These are legitimate objections. Who could dispute that time spent actually in front of a buyer selling is better spent than conducting an analysis? But if the analysis isn't done before the buyer contact, the sales presentation could be a fiasco and the time spent there counterproductive – not just a waste of time, but actually doing damage to the buyer's perception of the company's professionalism.

Getting the budget released for MR can be a serious source of aggravation. The money can be given grudgingly, or not enough may be given. Or if it's given, the expectations that come with it are unrealistic. The manager commissioning marketing research in this kind of situation needs to manage those expectations carefully. No one can predict or guarantee the unqualified success of an MR exercise. But if you don't ask you won't learn.

One way to ease the strain on the corporate treasury is to join a multi-client study, set up either by an MR agency or by a government or trade association body. This is a useful way of saving cost. It's usually possible to negotiate the inclusion of questions specific to your organization's needs into the study, so there's a double benefit: – the general overview applicable to the overall industry and the specific questions on the company.

SCOPE OF MARKETING RESEARCH

In certain countries there are codes of conduct for MR investigators. For example, an agency may talk to 50 buyers on your behalf and be able to list their organizations in the report, but if it quotes from the interview records, it cannot attribute the quote to a named buyer or company. That can be seen by some executive as a limiting factor and as unnecessarily scrupulous.

But there are many ways other than specially commissioned market research in which you can get market information, particularly if it relates to a market in which your organization already operates. All of the following can provide information on different areas of the market.

Buyers/prospects

- sales presentations to prospects

- training courses for the company's buyer-customers

- advertising response from prospects/buyers

- direct mail response from prospects/buyers

- service call-outs to buyer premises

- deliveries to customer premises

- frequency and nature of requests to quote

- the organization's own invoicing records

- factory visits by buyers

- the process of supplier quality assessment

- EDI links to buyer's production build schedules

- complaints from buyers.

Competitors

- competitor product brochures

- competitor annual reports

- competitor price lists
- competitors' kit.

Distributors
- sales planning meetings
- invoice records.

General marketing information
- exhibitions
- media relations
- trade journals
- press articles
- television and radio programmes
- market reports
- books

TRICKS OF THE TRADE

○ *Marketing research, carefully purchased is worth the investment; puts you ahead of your competitors; can help you learn about your company as well as the market; is an essential part of buyer communications; is the inbound aspect of the communications activity of every organization.*

○ *Data generated by MR activity, whether free text reports or numerical data from accounts records, should be blended with all other market-relevant data in the buyer information system.*

○ *If you pay peanuts, you get monkeys – but invest in quality marketing research, and you'll get substantial rewards.*

○ *This chapter has been about taking the market apart. Using a simple framework, the five Cs, any market can be analyzed in such a way that the key business issues are identified.*

○ *The five Cs are: context, customers, competitors, critical success factors, company.*

○ *This analysis forms the basis for strategic thinking, which is dealt with in chapter five, 'Getting the strategy Right', and chapter six, 'Managing Buyer Relationships'.*

Chapter two deals with the buying function, exploring the composition of the typical purchasing department and the dynamics of its relationship with other departments, notably quality and engineering. Chapters three and four examine the buying process and buyer's needs respectively. These three chapters on buyers represent an attempt to understand in considerably more detail one of the five Cs, namely, customers, the most important players in the market.

2

the buying function

In order to build a relationship with the buyer you need to thoroughly understand their structure, organization and individual behaviour. You need to know who to approach and how. Relationships can't begin until you're talking to the right person with the right message.

introduction

In any business development activity there's an essential need to understand and have an appreciation of the buyer. Where the business-to-business market is unique is that the buyer and specifiers of today are highly trained individuals. They are technically and commercially astute, and have a great deal of knowledge of the product in question and the various suppliers for that product/commodity. Underestimating the buyer results in poor communication, which leads to a business relationship that goes nowhere fast.

The buying role has become much more dynamic and so often the buyer's increase in professionalism, skill and ability isn't being matched by the marketer. It's time to consider closely the buyer's role, and develop a clear understanding of the buyer's function, priorities and organization. Obviously, all companies are structured differently, but the essence of how they operate follows similar lines.

The buying function centres around the purchasing department and its activities. It holds sourcing and purchasing responsibilities and, in recent years, we have seen the introduction of new strategies and thinking that have increased the role of the purchasing team in a structured and logical way. This has in turn led to a need for the buying function to align itself more closely with other functions within the organization. This has increased buyers' knowledge and assisted in the development of their skills. As a result of their closer association with other departments, influence can be solicited from those departments.

Through a greater understanding of the buyer's role and function, we can be better prepared for our dealings with him or her. Rather than being an obstruction, we can start to see how we can 'assist' and work in partnership with the buyer. If the buyer is partnership sourcing should not we be partnership developing? Working to develop the partnership for our benefit. Having identified the buyer's role and function, we should be aware of the communication skills and tailor our approach to them.

the sourcing/purchasing function

Where does sourcing end and purchasing begin? Many companies refer to 'partnership sourcing', though it may be better referred to as 'partnership purchasing', as you, as the supplier, are working in partnership so they purchase your product. The sourcing process is the buyer operating a process that will highlight and evaluate a number of potential suppliers. From this process a supplier is appointed and the buyer begins his or her role of purchasing.

The aim is to buy the highest quality products for the least cost global supply route. However, there are a number of other criteria that the buyer has to ensure are met. A low-cost product of acceptable quality isn't such a good prospect if the buyer has to agree to taking three months stock at a time, particularly if the purchased item represents a high value in relation to the final product.

In today's enviroment the emphasis is on the buyer controlling costs rather than merely negotiating prices (see Figure 2.1 overleaf). The strategies and structures are such that the buyer aims to work 'in partnership', to secure the best deal from the suppliers and ensure some form of cost stability and cost reduction. Increasingly, the estimation of the purchasing function is rising. The importance of the function is continually highlighted in today's cost-cutting environment. Without a successful purchasing function a company can look forward to high costs, high inventories and below par products. This leads to the company having to sell its products at higher prices, which leads to losing market share and customers. This in turn leads to less cash available for product development, research, marketing and customer service, reduced profits and eventually losses.

The knock-on effect of a poor purchasing function is recognized by all companies within all industry sectors. A successful purchasing organization can save a company significant costs, and it can also improve cash-flow by improved stock control and logistics. In essence it can make cash available and increase profits.

Figure 2.1

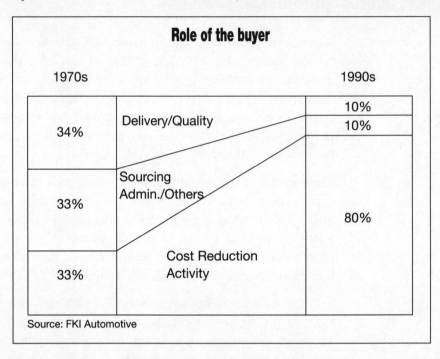

Source: FKI Automotive

Your company's purchasing function, whether small or large, is exactly the same as any other. It affects the profitability and cash-flow of the company. It can determine whether or not your product is manufactured on time, to the right specification and to the right quality standard. Too often the marketing and purchasing functions within companies are adversarial. In it's simplest form these two departments have significant control over the cost price and selling price of your company's products. By working in unison they can decrease costs, whilst looking to increase margins. It's vital that you know who the purchasing people are, their role and responsibilities, to engage their help and support in meeting the price that makes you, as the marketer, competitive.

purchasing departments

A typical purchasing department would be structured as shown in Figure 2.2.

Figure 2.2

Purchasing department organization

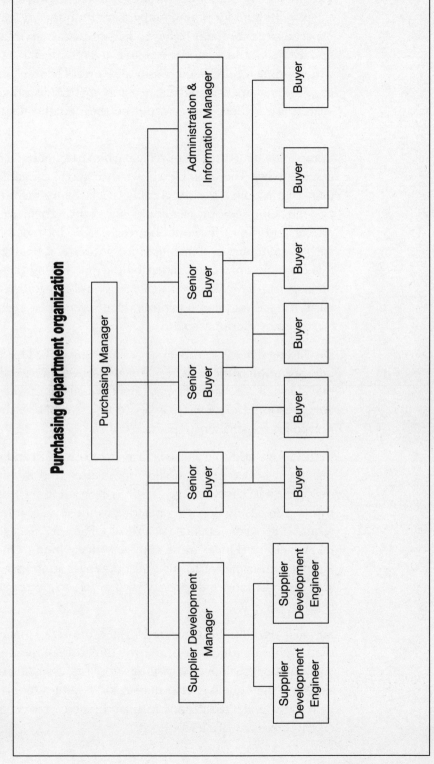

The number of personnel within the department varies in relation to the requirement for bought-in parts and sundries. Though you would expect a large company to have a large purchasing department, it may not always be the case. For example, a large metal pressing company, whose primary purchased commodity would be steel, may not have as large a department as a smaller company that distributes automotive spare parts, where there would be the demand for a vast array of products.

Companies structure the purchasing department into specific areas of responsibility. The example shown in Figure 2.2 could be for a company that requires the purchasing of plastic, rubber and metal components. One senior buyer could take responsibilities for plastics and rubber and the other could be responsible for metals and sundries, such as stationery and maintenance products. Capital expenditure, in this example, may be retained by the purchasing manager. It is not unusual for the managers to take responsibility for the purchasing of parts, services or plant/equipment that represent a high proportion of the company's annual spend.

Purchasing departments will sometimes appoint a buyer to take specific responsibility for working on new projects or identifying new suppliers. It may be that the department is structured with senior buyers being responsible for all their key suppliers, while the buyers take responsibility for smaller suppliers.

In the above example we also have an information and administration manager who has responsibility for the internal communication of the purchasing department. This role is becoming increasingly popular within purchasing departments, due to the level of information that's required to be maintained, as a result of activity such as global sourcing, which introduces more supplier information to the department. Supplier information forms and quotation support documentation also bring in more information which has to be registered and collated.

Supplier development managers will often now operate as a part of the purchasing function. Under the direction of the purchasing manager, their role will involve visiting suppliers, assessing their capability, assessing their quality performance and issuing a report that will highlight the supplier as acceptable, unacceptable or acceptable as long as certain measures are introduced.

As well as the sourcing and purchasing of goods and services the purchasing department will generally maintain responsibility for the materials management. This is concerned with the flow of materials into an organization. Schedulers or planners may be appointed to issue the orders and schedules, and plan the flow of incoming goods. This role may be within the realm of the buyer's activity. Some organizations will have the purchasing manager reporting to a materials manager, who has an inventory manager also reporting to him or her. The inventory manager will then have a logistics team reporting to him or her.

sourcing strategies

In today's environment of just-in-time and total quality management philosophies buyers are ensuring that their sourcing activities identify suppliers who become an integral part of the material flow process. In taking this stance, the drive towards ever closer relationships between companies and their vendors is continual. Reverse marketing, where the buyer 'sells' the concept of supplying his or her company, is a two-way communication process that sees the buyer imparting far more knowledge to suppliers than was the case in the days of adversarial buying and selling.

This approach is in line with the global and partnership sourcing strategies as implemented by most companies. The practice of global sourcing allows suppliers to be identified that provide opportunities to develop, in partnership, products and material flow processes that meet the JIT/TQM demand of the buying company.

GLOBAL SOURCING Global sourcing is a means of identifying the least cost global supplier, whilst retaining an acceptable level of quality and service. Purchasing departments that fully embrace global sourcing are prepared to have a virtual open-door policy towards information from potential suppliers. They need to develop a greater understanding of global economics and trust their judgement in appointing suppliers who aren't necessarily local.

The buyer's research is a key element as it provides the details of potential suppliers. The success or failure of global sourcing is very dependent upon the buyer securing quotations from as broad a base as possible. The buyer who is limited to only a small number of companies isn't striving to identify real opportunities. The process of securing quotations generates competition on a large scale for the existing and potential suppliers. There may then be a second round of quotes with a smaller number of companies and target prices may be set.

Organizations will take a team approach to global sourcing, particularly where companies have a number of international offices and associated purchasing departments. Obviously, these companies can reap the immediate benefit of scales of economy as long as other criteria can be met such as JIT supply. These companies also have the benefit of being able to use their various offices to maximize the research and establish a wide selection of initial potential suppliers. This team approach will allow for the activities to be co-ordinated between the various offices and will keep the global sourcing programme focused. Remember that the driving force behind global sourcing is cost reduction.

The identification of competitive and capable suppliers, via global sourcing, allows the partnership sourcing process to commence. In England the Confederation of British Industry and the Department of Trade and Industry define partnership sourcing as:

a commitment by customers/suppliers regardless of size, to a long-term relationship based on clear, mutually agreed objectives to strive for world class capability and competitiveness.

In embracing partnership sourcing, again the buyers are embracing a cost reduction strategy. The linking of the two companies allows for closer co-operation in all activities that provides a better service for both the companies concerned. Key advantages can clearly be identified as:

● the relationship enhances the product development role, with the supplier playing a more integrated role in assisting in the design and development of the part that it will ultimately supply. This level of involvement also allows products to be developed at a faster rate than if a company tried to design all the varying aspects itself

● by working together on quality issues and through joint identification of areas of concern, a better quality performance can be achieved

- long-term agreements allow for the planning of a number of issues by both parties.

Benefits specific to the buyer are:

- a proportion of design and development costs are carried by the supplier

- economies of scale

- on-time deliveries and an improved level of service

- improved quality

- assurance of supply.

And the supplier benefits through:

- assurance of supply

- accurate scheduling

- business development advantage

- payments on time

- assistance with quality issues.

The supplier's costs are known to the buyer, as is the margin, though not necessarily the net profit. A realistic return gives the supplier profit so that it can continue to develop as a company and fund activities such as research, a design/development team and new plant/equipment. Joint action is taken to reduce costs, and this benefits both parties, who can then be more competitive. The buyer knows that the supplier is being fair in its pricing and this encourages the development of further business.

Communication in partnership sourcing

If the buyer does a good job of communicating needs to the supplier, and the supplier does a good job of communicating needs to the buyer, they can mutually work out all the opportunities before they become problems.

The above, taken from *Purchasing in the 21st Century* by John E. Schorr, highlights the importance of communication in the partnership environment. Throughout the buyer/supplier relationship, communication, from the very start, is an important factor. Good communication is critical. By good we mean open, honest and continual. If either party has alternative plans to those being openly discussed then eventually they will be found out and the whole relationship will be in jeopardy.

The buyer, scheduler, supplier quality assurance (SQA) engineer and the development engineer are all key players in communicating with the supplier's sales, quality and technical personnel. Communication will be through numerous means such as telephone, faxes, questionnaires, quotations and drawings. This communication results in the supplier being treated, and feeling, as a part of the company.

WATCH OUT!

The communication process is geared towards keeping the seller selling. The more you push your company forward and try to secure the business the more vulnerable you become to making 'just one more' concession. It is difficult to turn the tables and keep the buyer selling when you are competing against a large number of companies, yet at the same time you cannot afford to stop selling.

the purchasing department's relationship with other departments

The purchasing function concerns itself mainly with the sourcing of goods and services, whilst also applying itself to materials management. A good purchasing department will work closely with a number of other functions within the company. Materials management may be handled by a separate inventory department and it's necessary for these departments to work in unison.

The purchasing department is heavily involved in other divisions of its company, and the impact that it has within any company in maintaining low costs and supporting other functions is increasingly more prominent. Without the purchasing function you, me and everyone else would not survive in the commercial world.

LOGISTICS/ MATERIALS MANAGEMENT

Associated to the purchasing function, these areas of product control will often start with the buyer. They'll be responsible for ensuring that the supplier that they've selected can supply according to their requirements. Whatever the supply basis, the buyer has to initiate you into his or her requirements. The buyer who has good control of the supply logistics and through-flow of materials, maintains a lower inventory and reduces the cash-flow element of the bought-in goods. There may be a demand for 'just-in-time' (JIT) deliveries of which the buyer should advise you before any supply contracts are entered into.

Just-iln-time (JIT) This has become a much abused term and clarification should always be sought as to what the buyer exactly means. Just-in-time is a means of satisfying the supply requirements, in line with a company's material-flow process, in a cost-efficient manner for both parties. To one company it may mean a delivery every four hours, whereas to another it could mean every seven days. Many suppliers still balk at a requirement for JIT deliveries. Don't fear it. Once described as Japanese Inspired Terror, JIT should be looked at as a means of economical supply that reduces the amount of stock you hold and allows you to reduce your work in progress and implement a JIT philosophy throughout your own company.

Synchronous supply This is only possible for those companies sited very near to their customer, as it effectively involves a company in producing the component in sync with the customer's production, to arrive at its plant for immediate use as soon as it's required. In general this will necessitate several deliveries per day direct to the assembly line. Though this is an ideal arrangement, the practicalities for many companies of organizing their plants is obviously uneconomical and unviable. It's a method of supply that will be seen with only high-value products, in high demand and particularly where there are a number of variants. A typical example would be a car seat plant where the seats come in a variety of trim and where there's a constant demand for the product from the car manufacturing plant.

Consignment stocking In this instance, the supplier maintains a level of stock, within a consignment stock area that's within the locality of the buyer. Locality may mean within the USA if you're supplying an American company from France, or it may mean within New York if you are a supplying company based in California. The consignment stock is, generally, maintained within the warehouse of a third party that sells such services, although it may also be warehousing owned by the buyer's company, possibly off-site but within the region of its plant. The buyer then calls off and takes whatever volume is required and notifies the supplier who then invoices accordingly. This arrangement is ideal for companies that need to facilitate the buyer's JIT supply requirements, but are based overseas.

LOGISTICS The logistic functions within an organization can be a part of the responsibilities of a number of departments, such as production, inventory and goods out. Purchasing has to have a clear understanding of the overall logistics and how it affects their department. It may be that production is planning a major increase in volumes. This could have a number of side affects for purchasing:

- a supplier, as selected by purchasing, won't be able to meet the demand so there'll be a need to identify a second source

- with increased volumes there may be an opportunity for purchasing to renegotiate new prices from the supplier

- it may use re-useable packaging, more of which will have to be sourced and ordered to cope with the increased volumes

- there may be a need to fund an additional press tool or mould, as the existing tool wouldn't be able to produce the required weekly requirements

- it may use an outside carrier for its products and the increased use of the carrier could lead to purchasing negotiating a new contract

- it may need to purchase a new delivery vehicle.

Well thought out logistics and material management are fundamental to successful purchasing. Increasingly the emphasis is on controlling and monitoring this area to release additional cash and not allow cash to be tied up in massive stocks.

QUALITY When sourcing products the quality capability of the supplier has to be assessed. The quality department therefore becomes an important support function to the purchasing department. Supplier quality assurance (SQA) engineers may be an integral part of the purchasing department, though often they'll report to a quality assurance manager who in turn could report to the materials manager.

In today's marketplace, the buyer won't make the purchase until a supplier has been quality audited. Often the buyer will visit the plant with the SQA engineer and together they'll asses your company. The engineer is a major influencer on the buyer, and working in close association, the buyer's knowledge on quality matters will advance at a quicker rate than those of his or her marketing counterpart.

ENGINEERING The engineering/technical/design department is another division that will work closely with purchasing. The products that require purchasing will often stem from the work that the engineering department is carrying out. It will establish the need and provide drawings and specifications. It must then impart the requirement to the relevant buyer and ensure that he or she fully understands what is required. As with the quality function, purchasing personnel also learn from the close co-operation with engineering.

Without a full technical understanding of the product that's being developed the buyer is unable to commence sourcing. Therefore, the buyer gains a thorough technical appreciation before discussing the part with any suppliers. This immediately puts the buyer at an advantage. As buyers develop within certain commodity areas, their expertise is developing, and as they gain exposure to a number of suppliers, they gleam the technical strengths from each supplier and this in turn increases their expertise.

ACCOUNTS Invoices that are received have to be verified by purchasing before payment is made. It needs to confirm that the order was placed and delivered according to the requirements specified. The relationship between the purchasing and accounts departments is an obvious one but in the future their links may become stronger as EDI becomes utilized not only as a direct ordering system but also as an invoice and payment system. This will simplify and quicken transactions.

the buyer's career

The portrayal of the go-getting and dynamic salesman, in his company car and earning bonuses, overshadows the dynamism of the buyer. Buyers are generally well educated, with good learning ability, and tough negotiators, who unlike their sales counterparts don't let emotions play a part of the sales/buying process. In fact recent surveys show that over 70 per cent of buyers view a formal education as necessary to do their job well. Many buyers receive ongoing training far beyond what the average sales/marketing person receives, with 85 per cent of buyers supporting the need for such ongoing training.

The natural progression for a buyer is to aim for a senior buyer's role then on to a purchasing manager's position. As the buyer progresses through the department he or she will have increasing exposure to other disciplines within the organization. The buyer may take more control of logistics, responsibility for stock control and supplier quality assurance.

Companies are taking on fresh graduates for a 'purchasing career', full of ambition and drive. Indeed, what was often seen as a solitary and dour field is now a dynamic and thrusting function that's an integral part of any company and one that can significantly affect the success of that company.

priorities and goals

So often purchasing personnel refer to their cost-saving targets, which include supplier reduction programmes. Fundamentally, these are the two key priorities that affect you the most.

The business-to-business market is increasingly demanding with regard to cost reduction. Existing suppliers are being asked to reduce costs through increased efficiency and improved sourcing. They are being pressurized by potential new suppliers seeking the opportunity to quote, who so often look to low margins as a way of 'getting in the door'. The buyer has a target and will strive to achieve that target, as long as a number of other criteria, such as quality, can be met.

Many new contracts are signed that require annual cost reductions. This helps the buyer to meet future targets and satisfy the demands of the employer. The buyer should, though doesn't always, look at their service to the supplier. The buyer who looks to reduce costs from existing suppliers whilst issuing erratic schedules, late payments, sudden technical changes and volumes far below the original quoted for isn't well positioned to argue for cost reductions. However, this won't prevent the buyer asking, and where the cost to change suppliers is minimal they may seek another supplier who's unaware of the associated problems.

Supplier reduction strategies are a way of developing stronger links with suppliers and a method of cost reduction. They reduce costs through less administration and by securing a cheaper source, as a result of increased volumes from the selected supplier. On products that require a high level of assembly, supplier reduction often sees a number of suppliers dropping down the supply chain, as the assembler moves to a more integrated systems supply. Supplier reduction is often linked in with such activities as global sourcing and partnership sourcing, as the buyer needs to harness opinion and facts from a number of existing and potential suppliers to ensure that he or she rationalises to those suppliers who best meet the criteria.

Other areas where buyers are likely to be targeted include supply logistics, where, in order to increase their own efficiency and reduce inventory, they look to suppliers to switch from, say, a weekly delivery to three deliveries per week. This cost-saving strategy for them is an additional cost burden to you, as is so often the case with buyer's cost reduction strategies. The supplier that benefits as a result of supplier rationalization programmes may see its turnover increase, but the margins will be squeezed further as a result of economies of scale that are enforced. For a preferred supplier there'll also be increasing demand for engineering and design input, which again adds to your costs.

So with the buyer's priorities and goals centred around cost reduction, the additional cost burdens on the supplier must be carefully considered. Every supplier has room for improvement, and without a process of continuous improvement many companies will begin to suffer in today's market. Increased efficiency works for the benefit of the supplier and the customer.

performance assessment

The key level on which a buyer is assessed is the bottom-line figure, i.e. cost savings. This has an immediate affect on profits and cash-flow and is very visual, but this will not be the only criterion.

Buyers may also be targeted and assessed on their achievement of supplier reduction targets, on their implementation of a global sourcing strategy and on the performance of their selected suppliers. The need for buyers to be good administrators is also highlighted by the fact that many companies asses their buyer's ability in this area. This would take into consideration areas such as scheduling, invoice approval, and general maintenance and records. Some companies may choose to evaluate their research methods and awareness of new companies, and whether any of these have brought any benefits to the company. The relationship of the buyer with other departments and the suppliers may be taken into account through securing their opinions, generally via questionnaires.

Buyers' performances are measured on a number of levels. We can assist them in their careers, through clear communication, quality service and products which provide them with all the necessary information and support. Remember, we are here to work in partnership with the buyer.

decision-makers

Every member of the purchasing department likes to play a role within the purchasing decision. However, it's fundamental to the selling and marketing process to know who the decision-makers are and who are the right people for you to be communicating with. The buyer may indicate that he or she makes the decisions but, the buyer may have to refer the decision on a particular commodity to a senior buyer or purchasing manager.

By understanding the structure of the purchasing department you can start to understand who the decision-makers are and their areas of responsibilities. The purchasing manager who has a large number of buyers is unlikely to make any direct purchasing decisions, unless there's a requirement on a particular commodity that represents an exceptionally high value of the final product. For example, a manufacturer of catalytic converters may have all the materials purchased by the buyers except for the precious metals that are required by the converter, which are sourced by the purchasing manager as they represent some 80 per cent of the total value of that component.

The influencers are those people who have a major input into the decision-making process and whose opinion is sought and respected by the buyer. Often these will take the shape of engineer, designers and/or SQA engineers. Personalities matter, and relationships between some buyers and, say, engineers may not be as good as you think, so the influencer may not exact as much influence as at first appeared.

Sometimes it's more beneficial to appeal to the influencer in the first instance than to the actual decision-maker. Again it's important to understand the buyer and the relationship with other functions. You need also to be aware of also the relationship between buyers, influencer and their existing suppliers. A supplier may have a good relationship with a buyer, but the engineer may think that the supplier is limited in its capabilities and offers little to technical discussions. On the other hand a quality assurance engineer may enthuse about the existing supplier's exemplary record in providing the best quality products and about SPCs, FMEAs and the merits of Taguchi, whereas the buyer has had enough of the supplier's continual push for increased prices.

Identifying the weak link is not an easy process, but by understanding the buyer's company structure you can identify those personnel who may have an effect on your product. However, remember that it's the buyer who will actually buy your product so don't alienate him or her by liaising extensively with other departments, without informing him or her of what's happening.

Meetings that involve the different functions should be sought as they'll highlight the inter-departmental relationships and provide a clear indication of who the major influencers are. It'll also show you the strength of the relationship between the influencer and buyer.

TRICKS OF THE TRADE

Plant visits that involve the buyer plus an influencer are useful in helping to identify the strength of the buyer/influencer relationship. At some point the two will be separate and the opportunity can then be taken to glean information from either party on an individual basis. This could highlight that the SQA engineer may be uncertain of aspects of your processes, yet the buyer is adamant that an order will be placed, as your cost structure is very competitive. The converse could be that the SQA engineer is very impressed by your quality processes, equipment and standards yet the buyer believes that your low-cost structure cannot be maintained. Either way you have established a rapport and have at least one contact who'll be supportive. Work with them to not only to secure their support but to identify concerns of any of the influencers/buyers. Once a concern is identified measures can then be taken to counter the concern.

buyer's communication skills

A good buyer will be an excellent communicator: clear and concise. As previously identified, for partnership sourcing, one of the key factors is the need for constant communication. As their function is to buy the highest-quality product at the lowest price whilst receiving an excellent service, buyers have to remain impartial and logical in their selection of suppliers. To achieve this, buyers will develop an array of techniques and tactics.

THE TECHNIQUES

Like a salesperson, the buyer has an array of techniques. Often this appears to be centred around '1,001 ways to say no'. The truth, however, is less cynical and highlights the differences between the emotional process of selling and the more logical and precise process of business-to-business purchasing. This doesn't mean that buyers are cold, robotic individuals devoid of emotion. Indeed, the successful purchaser gains plenty of job satisfaction in knowing that he or she has selected the right supplier, and bought in a cost competitive product of the highest quality from a company eager to impress with its technical capability, service and commitment.

How many marketers reading this can, hand on heart, claim that they truly believe that regular training is necessary to do their job. Surveys show that in excess of 85 per cent of purchasing personnel actually believe in on-going training. This reflects the professional approach of many buyers and the continuous improvement philosophy that so many of them have embraced.

The age-old technique of playing one supplier against another has generally given way to more sophisticated techniques, though the end result is the same. You're competing, playing, for a share or all of the business. The benchmark that buyers use will either be the existing supplier or, for new products, other potential suppliers. They'll make notes and compare costs, equipment, past performance and technical ability. They'll want to know your company's size in turnover, number of employees and profits. Your future strategy and investment plans will be discussed, and management as well as product quality will be assessed. Your company's mission statement and the operator on the factory floor will be analyzed.

All this is a form of failure mode effect analysis (FMEA). The question buyers have to ask themselves is what will happen if I use this supplier. They then have to go through a process of identifying weaknesses. Bear in mind, that to get to this stage will often take an awful lot of patience and determination from you, particularly if you're a potential new supplier, because buyers don't want to spend too much time on new suppliers, as time is money and they are trying to reduce costs not add to them.

Possibly the biggest advantage that buyer's have is their knowledge of your competitors. Buyers' exposure to a large variety of companies always gives them the advantage of knowledge, through the experiences of others. They can identify the strengths and weaknesses of each supplier, using this to their advantage. They know your competitors, far better than you can ever hope to. This is particularly true in today's age of open book policies, where the supplier reveals all to the buyer.

Not only do buyers have the price that they will buy at, but they also have the costs that go together to make that price. From this they can compare companies and identify the efficiencies of each company within their respective buying, production, finishing, assembling, packaging and delivery operations. Their knowledge will then be further enhanced when they visit the plant. Areas of future development and investment are discussed, so they already know where your competitors are going.

**TRICKS OF
THE TRADE**

○ *Gain information from the buyer.*

○ *It's hard to gather all the information you would like to on your competitors. Your relationship with buyers can yield some useful information.*

○ *Always listen if they should ever bring a competitor's name into a conversation. Learn your competitors' weaknesses, not to disparage them but to know which of your benefits to highlight.*

○ *Learn their strengths to avoid highlighting these product features.*

Many marketers fall down by not realizing their own weaknesses and limitations. Product and company strengths are the reasons that the marketer exists. Marketers are optimistic by nature, always looking for the positive elements. When trying to analyze your company's weaknesses be brutal and honest. Gather information from employees at all levels within the company. Allow people the freedom to criticize and then take corrective measures to counter these weaknesses. Then, if a buyer expresses any concern, you can assure him or her that you're taking measures to change things. This shows a pro-active company willing to follow a continuous improvement philosophy.

NEGOTIATING TACTICS

Often the main focus of negotiations is the price. Other elements that are often subject to negotiation are delivery schedules, payment terms and packaging; all of these have a bearing on cost for both parties. Today, many buyers try to approach negotiations with a win-win attitude, particularly on sole supply items. This approach basically sees both parties co-operating for the benefit of one another so that the negotiation has two winners and no losers.

The first element of successful negotiation is control of the procedure. Buyers understand this and will try to dominate the negotiations. The first advantage that they will go for is territorial. There's a psychological advantage for the meeting(s) to take place at their premises, just as there's an advantage for negotiations to take place at your premises, if possible. You may also be aware that, when negotiations involve a group of people, the buyers will try to keep the other party members separated. It weakens the collective strength of the pack.

The buyer will be well prepared and will let you, initially, do most of the talking and present your case. This is intentional. The buyer is waiting for you to talk yourself into concessions, some of which were never the original intention. Many buyers have got silence down to a fine art. That uneasy moment where you've finished what you wanted to say but feel the buyer isn't convinced. Seconds appear to have lasted minutes and away you go talking yourself into submission. No end of sales trainers advise sales personnel to shut up. Silence is an artform that's being perfected by the buying profession.

Another area where buyers excel is in the Mr Spock approach to emotions. By avoiding emotional reactions, whilst stating their case and whilst listening to yours, it becomes much harder to identify weak spots and areas where they may make concessions. Ultimatums, of the take it or leave it variety, don't occur, though it may feel otherwise, because in doing so the buyer closes the door on the negotiation. The buyer may have secured all the concessions that he or she wanted, but the door has been closed on any further concessions and, effectively, on the relationship. Professional buyers will achieve all they want to from the negotiations but will leave the relationship intact for further concessions, some of which you may not even have though of, yet!

You've won the order and have done a pleasing job in persuading the buyer. It's a fact that many buyers will allow you to persuade them to buy. The satisfaction of having made the sale will leave you amenable to 'just one more' concession to finalise the deal.

working relationships with buyers

The success of the sale and the continued development of the business rely purely on your company's relationship with the buyer. In an ideal environment, there would be one contact for the buyer to deal with, though this is rarely possible. For example, a sales team may be supported by a telesales operation, the technical salesperson may be supported by a design function, the products being supplied may require the support of technical and servicing personnel, and there's the receptionist who handles all incoming calls.

BUYER – THE IMMEDIATE EMOTION

So often companies refer to the customer, their customer interfacing staff, and their customer satisfaction programmes. Buyer is a much more immediate term and drives home clearly the purpose of the customer, which is to buy your goods and services. The word buyer immediately projects an image of money changing hands from the buyer's company to your company. Customers are people who we see in the supermarket: tame, inoffensive and nothing to do with us. So at work customers are people we *have* to look after we don't necessarily respect or have any emotional ties with them. We understand buying, we do it ourselves all the time, we give money to people for clothes, food and drink. Parting with money is an emotional process, we have worked hard for it. We want buyers to buy from us, moving money from their company into our company. They keep us employed, they affect our bonus, our future – we *want* them to buy from us. Employees who *want* things to be achieved will be more enthusiastic and keen to please the buyer rather than those who feel obliged to.

WATCH OUT!

Relationships should never become too familiar as this clouds the real purpose of the relationship; you're a supplier selling your goods and services to a buyer. Once the relationship becomes too familiar meetings become unproductive, phone calls are made for no real purpose and eventually the buyer goes elsewhere to that nasty company that keeps selling him or her things. On the other hand relationships should never become too disparate. The lack of warmth buyers feel can leave them feeling uncomfortable when they need to contact you. They would rather contact the other supplier or even invite a new supplier in. The relationship does not allow for a good base to develop business further, nor does it allow a level of trust to be established.

Earlier, buyers' commercial needs were discussed. Being able to understand what a buyer needs, emotionally, from a business relationship is also key to developing business. Some buyers like a cold relationship, where business is the only item on the agenda and meetings/discussions are curt and to the point. Others like to discuss mutual interests or personal agendas, as well as all the matters relating to the business. Some combine both, depending upon the issues to be discussed. The successful relationship is the one where the supplier's personnel can handle different buyers with a chameleon-like approach.

A strong relationship with a buyer should never be abused. On occasions, companies have pushed their luck too far because they have a good relationship with the buyer. In essence what they're doing is abusing that relationship, and like all relationships the buyer/marketer relationship is based on trust. Meetings, phone conversations, letters and faxes in general contain an element of action for either one or both parties to act upon. There exists a trust between the two that the quote will be on time, the goods will be delivered to schedule and the payments will be made according to terms. Without this basic level of trust the relationship is doomed.

The buyers who trust you are the ones who will confide in you. They can be a valuable source of information and guide you towards other opportunities.

We've already referred to buyers' desires not to become emotionally involved during the buying process. Their ideal is to remain in control, basing decisions on well thought out reason and logic. They have listened to your presentation and read your brochure, but are you really appealing to their emotions? Are you telling them benefits that they would expect anyway? Have the benefits of your company and product become merely features, as all companies have the same, more or less, benefits?

**TRICKS OF
THE TRADE**

○ *We have analyzed the buyers, and we know their priorities and targets. To achieve the sale there must be an effort to appeal to their emotions. Allow them to become emotionally involved in the buying and selling procedure.*

○ *Buyers are human. They want as much reward as possible for as little effort as possible. If you appeal to their emotions by identifying how your product/service can help them meet their targets, they become more amenable, listen more intently, and want to make a decision in your favour.*

Costs, quality, service and technical matters are all key areas that can help buyers achieve targets. So often, advancement within quality, service and engineering has a cost-saving or profit-making agenda for the buyer. This needs to be demonstrated to the buyer. It may be that you're a plastic moulding company that adds value to your products by offering sub-assembly services. What's the benefit to buyers? Doesn't this mean that they can increase their manufacturing costs without incurring the high costs of investing in their own plant and machinery, to carry out the subassembly in-house? Now we are appealing to their emotions and introducing cost savings, helping them to achieve their targets, advancing their careers and ensuring they're rewarded and applauded for their efforts.

By highlighting cost savings you're tackling the buyer with his or her most favoured subject. In some areas buyers may actually spend more for the sake of increasing profits, without necessarily reducing costs. For example, a car alarm system is sold by a car manufacturer. The system is cheap but sells very little due to reliability problems. A more expensive system is introduced that's more reliable. The car manufacturer sells more and makes a larger profit.

3

the buying process

A key feature of organisational buying behaviour is the often complex and lengthy decision-making process. This chapter takes you through the different steps of the buying process and shows how a trusting relationship can be developed between the marketer and buyer.

introduction

Fundamental to successfully developing your business is the need to clearly understand the various stages of the buying process. The business-to-business market, generally, has long drawn out procedures that aim to ensure the buyer secures the right product/commodity at an acceptable quality level and via the least-cost global supply route. The buying process will obviously vary from one market sector to the next and from company to company, though it's designed to ensure that all the necessary facts and figures are gathered before any decision is made. Once all the information is collated, the decision-maker can then make a decision with confidence, based on factual evidence. On your part, throughout the buying process your company needs to impart total confidence, in whatever contact you may have with the buying company.

The buyer's role could not be easier: ask for a quote, get a price and select the cheapest. Well let's try the process ourselves and leave business-to-business marketing for a second. Let's say you decide to buy a new sofa:

● *The need* – your present sofa has a spring sticking up and one of the armrests has dropped off

● *The specification* – the colour has to match existing decor and be able to seat three people

● *The sources* – you select a number of furniture stores to visit

● *The enquiry* – on visiting the stores you discuss your requirements with the sales assistants and identify:

   – several shapes: low backs with and without armrests; low backs with armrests level with the back; high backs with low, high and no armrests; sofas that go around a corner; some that have armrests, high at the back and low at the front; some that are very curved whilst others are very square; sofa beds

   – several different patterns: plain, stripes, circles, dots, paisley, etc.

   – several material types – leather, cotton, etc.

● *The quotation* – whilst at the stores you observe prices and request a quote for a specific style in a specific colour

- *The negotiation* – you revisit the store and negotiate the final price and delivery

- *The order* – you decide to place the order

- *The follow-up* – you phone to ensure that the sofa will arrive on the date agreed

- *The delivery* – you receive the sofa.

What you have just gone through is the buying process. So, we have an immediate appreciation of this process. In purchasing the buyer follows the same procedure but with a number of added difficulties and twists. For example, locating the sources won't be so easy. Would you have got the sofa cheaper if you'd shopped around a bit more? How often have you said 'I like that, where did you get it from?' and then gone on to ask 'Where is that?' Buyers have to make sure they are buying from the best and most competitive source and that they are familiar with all the potential sources.

In order to examine the buying process, we will follow the process, using a fictitious example, with a company called Sabig Industries, which is about to introduce a new product.

the need

Sabig has an engineering department, which has designed a new electric shaver, based on one of its existing designs, that requires a number of components. One of the main requirements will be the plastic moulded casing. The need has been established, and the most obvious prerequisites in purchasing is the establishment of a need. The need in this instance has been established by Sabig's engineering department. There are of course other circumstances that lead to the establishment of the need:

- New project/product – the need doesn't necessarily stem from engineering or research and development. Human resources may have a need for newspaper advertising space, marketing may have a need for marketing research, and production may have a need for new machinery.

- Cost reduction – often as a reactive measure due to price increase pressures. Purchasing raises the need, but it may also be a part of a global purchasing strategy.

- Problem with an existing supplier – the current supplier may have a poor quality performance or delivery record, or may be looking for a price increase. It may have become financially unstable or too reliant upon the buyer's company. It may not want to supply the product any more. Purchasing, quality or scheduling departments will establish the need.

- Increasing volumes requires more capacity – successful sales and marketing has increased demand and established the need

- Changing specification – the product may have to adapt to meet changing requirements or fashions or new legislation. Engineering, R&D and/or their customers establish the need.

- Existing tool to be replaced – this could either be due to wear and tear on the existing tool or as a result of an engineering change. The need is being generated either by engineering or quality departments.

the specification

With the new product design, Sabig's engineering department has drawn up the relevant specification for the buyer of plastic mouldings, who is Lynn King. This specification includes the drawings, material types, colour of material, logo design and colour, and the tolerances that the products should be moulded to. Without the specification, arising from the need, Lynn King is unable to commence the sourcing process. The more specification that she receives then the more selective she can be in her supplier selection criteria.

the sources

Sabig has suppliers located throughout the world and operates a global sourcing policy. The buyer collates information from an array of sources, with the minimum criterion of some form of recognized quality certification such as ISO. Lynn King has an array of potential sources that can be collated from:

- existing suppliers

- past quotations

- presentations received

- brochures

- trade journals

- directories

- trade organizations

- exhibitions

- advertisements

- the buyer's professional body

- colleagues

- buyers within other companies.

In many cases, further additional qualifying criteria will be initially used to ensure a manageable list, particularly where potential suppliers could run into their hundreds, if not thousands. The buyer at Sabig, as well as requiring some form of recognized quality certification, ideally requires suppliers who have pad printing facilities, as the case to the electric shaver will feature Sabig's logo. Plant list information is also of interest as companies that are geared up to supply large mouldings only won't be able to be competitive.

Again, to ensure a manageable list, where the information shows a lack of the qualifying criteria, unless the company is personally known to Lynn King, that company won't be selected as a potential supplier.

This highlights the need for companies to ensure that wherever they publicize and advertise their name, they impart all the key facts. Buyers want all the information that relates to capability. Whether or not you've any form of recognized quality certification; manufacturing processes and whether you have any secondary operations, such as assembly or packaging. Buyers like to attain some idea of size through figures such as number of employees, turnover and factory size. Full address and contact numbers with, ideally, names are required. Who your customers are is of interest; it highlights a certain capability and quality standard that may be of relevance.

EARNING TRUST Wherever your company name appears, ensure that the facts are indeed facts and not myths. If a brochure is slightly out of date amend it with a covering letter; if you're working towards ISO registration, state the fact but don't state it if you've no current plans to register.

A recently updated directory showed a company to be 'working towards ISO9002'. Four years before, the first edition of this directory showed the same company to be 'working towards ISO9002'. The fact that this appears, and that the company has been unable to achieve registration in four years, doesn't give the buyer any confidence whatsoever in that potential supplier.

○ *Honesty within your advertisements, brochures, presentations or wherever your name appears is the first step in earning the trust and respect of the buyer.*

TRICKS OF THE TRADE

GLOBAL SOURCING VERSUS SUPPLIER REDUCTION PROGRAMMES The process of global sourcing involves casting out a wide net and trawling in all the sources possible. By inviting more companies to quote, competition increases. In the face of this competition many companies will ignore the opportunities that come their way. They fail to understand why a company is collating so much information and obtaining so many quotes, and they see it as flying in the face of supplier reduction programmes. Cynically, it's treated as a means to drive down the price from the current supplier.

Firstly, are you afraid of competition? If so, how have you managed to survive in today's competitive markets? Secondly, we've already seen that global sourcing is indeed a cost-cutting exercise. Is your company not trying to reduce its costs? Thirdly, no buyer can source confidently unless he or she has all the relevant facts. To do so would mean that the buyer is potentially aligning his or her company with suppliers of a lower status or capability. A buyer, therefore, who responds negatively to a potential supplier's approach, due to a company policy of reducing the number of suppliers, is missing the point of global sourcing. The professional buyer will listen, to ensure that the small number of select suppliers is indeed the best for their requirements.

the enquiry

Having collated all the information on plastic moulding companies that met the initial criteria, Lynn King puts together a package that comprises:

- covering letter
- drawings and specifications
- request for quotation form
- quotation support documentation
- self-assessment/supplier profile forms.

The package is then forwarded to each company, with a deadline for the quotation. Since introducing its global sourcing policy, Sabig has established a number of key suppliers around the world and, though these are listed as preferred suppliers, when sourcing for new products it likes to involve a large number of companies. This lengthy exercise enables it to ensure that its preferred suppliers are still competitive, and that it isn't missing out on any technological advances or any new grant schemes, as introduced in various countries, such as assistance with tooling costs. The companies, on receipt of the new package, will then go though its contents.

COVERING LETTER   The covering letter basically outlines that Sabig is embarking on a new project and that it's inviting a number of companies to quote. The letter goes on to say that Sabig will be unable to accept quotations without the completion of the various forms. In this instance Lynn King has also chosen to reiterate the deadline.

DRAWINGS AND SPECIFICATIONS

The drawings provide dimensions of the products to be moulded and all the various specification details such as surface finishes, material and colour.

In some cases where specifications are lengthy, a number of additional items may be mentioned on a separate specification sheet. In other markets, such as market research or personnel selection, the specification will be a written request outlining the requirements.

REQUEST FOR QUOTATION FORM

This form is the official request form, and the reverse of the form has Sabig's general terms and conditions. This form provides key information such as quotation deadline, part numbers and volumes. In some cases these forms also have a target price, though in this instance Sabig hasn't included any.

With service industries, it's more likely that the covering letter will state any quotation deadline and any other relevant information, rather than include this form in the package.

QUOTATION SUPPORT DOCUMENTATION

Sabig's quotation support documentation (QSD) requested a complete breakdown of the component costs, including raw material, labour, process, packaging and transportation costs as well as a complete breakdown of the associated tooling costs. Increasingly, this is standard procedure for many companies, and generally quotes won't be considered further unless these forms are completed and returned.

Quotation support form - Sabig Industries

Supplier	Part no.	Dwg no.
Description	Volume per annum	

Supplier must complete the following information and return the quotation no later than _____

1. Procured parts

Part no./Description	Supplier country of manufacture	No. off	Unit cost
	Sub total (1)		

2. Materials

Description/Type/Size	Raw mat. cost	Gross	Net	%age Scrap	Component cost
			Sub total (2)		

3. Process (by operation)

	Sub con Y/N	Facility type	Shift patt	Labour cost	Facility cost	Component cost
				Sub total (3)		

Packaging/Pallet

Type of packaging	
Cost per box	
Cost per pallet	
No. of parts per box	
No par parts per pallet	
packaging per component cost	

Tooling Costs

Total tooling costs	
Tooling amortization (if applicable)	

Yearly price reductions

Year 2		%
Year 3		%
Year 4		%

Signed supplier
Date

4. Other costs

General overheads	
Capital depreciation	
R&D (specific to this part)	
Other (please specify)	
Profit	
Handling charges on procured parts	
Sub total (4)	

Tooling amortisatization (5)	
Sub total (5)	

6. Logistics

Delivery frequency	
Transport	
Packaging	
Pallet amortization	
Sub total (6)	

Total selling price (1)+(2)+(3)+(4)+(5)+(6)

Those companies that have ignored the quotation support documentation, are unlikely to be considered further as they're being a hindrance and not a help to the performance of Lynn King. Perhaps, if the quote is very competitive, she'll contact the quoting company, but as far as she's concerned she's having to do extra work. If she has to chase you for information now, will she have to chase you for products, if you become the supplier? As a potential supplier, the first chance that Lynn King has to asses your ability is in the supply of quotations, with all requested information.

The advantages and disadvantages of these forms

Suppliers' attitudes to quotation analysis forms vary and many still try to avoid them. This open-book approach is fundamental to developing a working partnership. The whole issue of disclosing your cost structure is one of trust, and in any partnership both parties must be able to trust one another. To understand the advantages and disadvantages of these forms there must be an appreciation of the aims of the buyer. So often companies view such information as a tool, to get the existing supplier to reduce its price. What they don't realize is that if the buyer was to use such a technique all that he/she would need is a price and not a complete cost breakdown.

These forms indicate within what areas your company has its strengths and weaknesses. It may be that you have competitive labour costs or run a very lean operation with minimal overheads or are effective in driving down the costs of raw material suppliers. By knowing where your competitive strengths are, the buyer and his technical or SQA engineer may be able to assist in improving the area where you're the least competitive. For example, the buyer may have negotiated a good price with a raw material supplier and where the buyer has suppliers, who require the same raw material, they may have the opportunity to take advantage of these prices.

○ *Through identifying your weaker areas, assistance may be provided in improving the competitiveness of these areas. This has the additional benefit of, potentially, increasing your profit on other business and your competitiveness.*

○ *A degree of trust and openness is immediately established that's reciprocated.*

○ *Any errors within the price calculation are highlighted to you by these forms and any corrections can then be made before submitting the quote.*

The disadvantage of quotation analysis forms is often highlighted as 'Putting all your cards on the table and showing your hand'. Welcome back to the adversarial approach as seen from 1960 to the early 1980s. Where purchasing has continually advanced in its process and function, so many companies have a dated and old-fashioned attitude towards business development. What are these companies afraid to show – that they are making a profit? Nobody is in business to lose money. From a buyer's viewpoint a supplier that loses money eventually falls into liquidation. This causes several problems for the buyer. He or she has to locate potential new suppliers, secure quotations, ensure quality standards can be met and in this haste the new supplier appointed may turn out to be unsuitable in the long term. Whilst going through this process stocks have been exhausted and the buyer's company is unable to satisfy its customers, who in turn decide to look elsewhere. The additional problems that the unsuitable new supplier has brought encourages the buyer's company's customers to appoint a new supplier and so it loses the business.

One negative statement raised by these forms is: 'I don't want the buyer to know how much profit I make.' Why not? Without a reasonable return the buyer is well aware that you will be unable to invest in new plant and equipment, R&D and general improvements to provide a better product and service to the buyer. Without the money to invest, the buyer realizes that the one step ahead technology and service required will never be there. If the buyer tries to squeeze your profit, ultimately he or she will have to resource, so they can save themselves additional work and accept your margins.

If you're making an inordinate profit on your product then you must be either uncompetitive or providing a unique product or service. In the former instance you'll obviously not be around for long as you'll inevitably lose business. In the latter case be careful of the consequences that could materialize. Other companies in an associated field will soon figure out the profits that you're achieving. They'll jump on the bandwagon and immediately set out to undercut you and gain market share. You will have to reduce your margin, but inevitably in such circumstances your operating costs won't be as low as they could have been. This will lead to you maintaining the same costs. This erosion of your profit margin will seem endless until you're in a loss-making situation and you begin to spend heavily to revamp the company and reduce costs. You don't believe it could happen to you? I'm sure that's what IBM thought.

IBM had a product that was far superior to its competitors, so much so that the only way that the competition could compete was through producing IBM-compatible systems. Its profits were vast. The competition could only try to erode IBM's market share by producing quality products but at a lower price. IBM continued to puruse opportunities within the mainframe industry, where margins were still good, and was complacent about its dominance of the market. However, the explosive growth within the PC market caught it out. Following a period of huge losses, IBM incurred expensive re-structuring costs as it tried to regain share in a market where it was once the undisputed leader.

Another negative comment raised by these forms is: 'I don't want them to give my competitors any idea of my very competitive raw material costs.' How do you know they are competitive? Sure, your supplier has promised you that its prices are competitive, but what does that mean? It may be that in reality you're actually paying more than any of your competitors. The fact is that you don't actually know.

An honest and open approach to these forms saves the buyer time and is reciprocated by an honest and open approach from the buyer.

FAST TRACK

SELF-ASSESSMENT/ SUPPLIER PROFILE FORMS Sabig uses these forms to give Lynn King an impression of your company's capabilities, strengths and weaknesses. As with the QSDs, without completion of these forms, you're making her job harder. Many companies supply a guide on how to complete the forms, which will always have some variation. Some companies will ask you to award yourself marks against certain questions, where as others may ask for a simple yes or no answer.

The profile that these forms provide will often form the basis of any future quality audits that may be carried out, so avoid any misrepresentation of the facts. In Sabig's case these forms are also accompanied by some notes as to how the forms should be completed and the scoring process as used by Sabig in the quality assurance audit.

the quotation

Sabig has seen your glossy brochure and has heard you espouse of the virtues of your company. This is the first enquiry you've received from Sabig, so in your haste to impress you write a price on a compliment slip and send it to the company. You don't hear anything from Sabig ever again. Are you surprised?

So often, companies that lavish money on excellent brochures, generate good impressions with their presentations, go on to ruin all their hard work through a lackadaisical approach, in responding to the first enquiry that they receive. The quotation deadline is missed, the quotation support documentation isn't completed and the self-assessment form is barely acknowledged.

Companies such as Sabig spend a lot of time and energy putting together enquiry packages. Every element of the package costs money. If you're unable to respect what they've done and spend time and energy in completing all the documentation in the proper manner, then don't expect them to go chasing you.

In your response to Sabig you've calculated the weights of the drawn components, which then allows you to calculate your quotation. You respond to Sabig within the deadline, providing all the information requested. Everything has been typed and the package is as presentable as your glossy brochure. You've faxed a summary of the quotation to Lynn King, advising her that the documentation is in the post.

EARNING TRUST

So often the first genuine opportunity that a company has to earn a
buyer's trust is during the quotation procedure. A deadline is set. You
fail to meet the deadline. The buyer's immediate response is that you
cannot be trusted. What should be almost a matter of procedure hasn't
been achieved. The first hurdle to gaining a new account has been
failed.

Make a note of quotation deadlines, enter it in your diary, on your PC
planner, or put it up on a whiteboard. Regrettably, many companies
are still unable to produce quotes on time. If, for whatever reason, the
quote will be late, advise the buyer and inform him or her of when
you'll be able to quote by and stick by that date. This isn't ideal – it's a
damage limitation exercise – but at least it's something. It's amazing
how many companies still fail to get quotations in on time and fail to
even contact the buyer. It may be that you've decided not to quote as
the part is unsuitable; if so, still inform the buyer. Don't ignore the
enquiry and then expect to receive any more enquiries from the buyer.

This is an age of advanced communications, so there's no logical
reason why a buyer should or cannot be informed. If the quotation is
requested along with a supplier profile and/or quotation support documentation then complete it and include it in your return.

EXAMPLE

Perseverance wins PSK the order

A plastic moulding company, Plastic Services Kolthoff Ltd (PSK), based in Ireland, received an unsolicited enquiry from a company it didn't know. It was asked to quote on a PVC product. However, its facilities weren't geared to moulding PVC, but rather than simply ignore the enquiry, it contacted the buyer and advised him accordingly. During the telephone conversation, PSK was able to establish that it did purchase other types of plastic mouldings and went on to give a clear indication of their capabilities. A letter and brochure were sent to the buyer concerned, and this was followed up by a telephone call.

Some eight weeks later PSK was invited to quote on a number of non-PVC plastic components. It completed the quotations and all the support documentation within the allotted time frame and faxed a summary to the buyer, forwarding the documentation by post. Over the following weeks it quoted on a number of other components and eventually landed its first order from this company, a major Japanese-owned European plant. If PSK had ignored the original, inappropriate enquiry, it wouldn't have won any orders. Through good communication, PSK was able to turn a situation with no obvious potential into an order-winning scenario. ○

the negotiation

Sabig now needs to collate all the information that it has received, make comparisons and enter into discussions and negotiations with competitive and capable companies.

THE COMPARISON

Sabig gathers all the information and initially compares prices. Those quotes that fall much higher than the majority of quotes will be put to one side, unless this includes any quotes from existing suppliers. In this circumstance Lynn King has to analyze the quotation support documentation to find out why an existing supplier's price is higher than a number of competitors. This could highlight a number of problems for the existing supplier and may see its existing business being put out to tender. Any company that uses a loss leader and then tries to recoup the loss through higher prices on additional business will soon be found out.

Sabig enters all the received costs into a PC on a spreadsheet format. This allows for an instant comparison between all the figures supplied. Once price comparisons are made, Lynn King compares the cost structures of the quoting companies. Through analysis of the costs, potential suppliers' differing efficiencies at different stages can be noted. It may be that one has half the packaging costs of another or uses less labour or has calculated a lower process cycle time. This throws up a number of questions for Lynn King. What if a company that is competitive but had high packaging costs were to re-source its packaging. Surely it could reduce the piece price? If that were your company and you responded by locating a cheaper source for your packaging the effect could be of benefit for all your products. The buyer won't give you figures from the other companies, but won't mind guiding you on where you are and where you aren't competitive.

Quotes that are far less than their nearest competitor are questioned by Lynn King. Does the supplier really understand the product required? Has it missed out any costs? In this scenario many buyers, unless they know the supplier well, will probably ignore the quotation. Suppliers that have a relationship with the buyer will probably be contacted to discuss the price.

From the spreadsheet Lynn King identifies eight companies that are showing competitive quotes, one of which is your company, Readon. Two companies with competitive quotes have supplied no additional information and she chooses to ignore these. Of the remaining six quoting companies, two are current suppliers.

The buyer now has a number of options on what to do. She may opt to ask the companies to requote. In doing so, a target price may be set. This target may be along the lines of the lowest quote received minus 5 per cent. Alternatively, if Lynn King had only received three competitive quotes she may have opted to visit each plant. As two quotes are from existing suppliers she could discuss this new requirement with only them.

In this instance, Lynn King further examines the costs and raises comments as shown in Figure 3.1.

Figure 3.1

Strengths and weaknesses of competitive companies		
Asholt	strengths	existing supplier good quality/delivery performance
	weaknesses	strong reliance upon Sabig taking the initiative
Beta	strengths	existing supplier very competitive pricing
	weaknesses	poor delivery performance against schedules
Cresta	strengths	within 20-mile radius of Sabig's plant enthusiasm
	weaknesses	low turnover for no. of employees
Readon	strengths	appear very capable technically have made cost/saving suggestions
	weaknesses	based overseas
Eston	strengths	cheapest quote on piece price and tooling low labour rate
	weaknesses	based overseas
Flaxo	strengths	very large company low material costs
	weaknesses	high overheads

The buyer may opt to go with an existing supplier, Asholt or Beta, that has given a competitive quote. This means that there are not the additional cost burdens that there would be in bringing in a new supplier. As a potential new supplier, it's up to you to sell the benefits of your company for the long term. In this instance, where Lynn King is adamant that an existing supplier will gain the business, you must make a decision as to whether or not you wish to continue to pursue this company. If the company buys an extensive amount of your type of product, then it may well be worth pursuing; if not, then think again. There may be a certain amount of prestige in supplying this company; may be it is part of a group and, in supplying this company, you could have potential access to other parts of the group. Whatever the reasons, evaluate the worth of this company to you – evaluate then act.

THE MEETING   Any company that invites you to discuss its requirements, either in person or by phone, after you have quoted for a particular part, obviously requires some additional insight to your company. This could possibly be of a technical nature, though it may be about of your cost structure and process. It may want to get a feel for the type of concessions that you're prepared to make in order to secure this business. Either way, the idea of this meeting/discussion in our example is to allow Lynn King to further evaluate your company and to explore your capabilities and the technical requirements of the parts in question.

Beta and Cresta make contact with Lynn King and both arrange meetings. The buyer then makes contact by phone with the other four companies and attempts to arrange meetings with each company at Sabig's premises. Asholt and Readon respond immediately and meetings are organized. Unfortunately, Eston appears to have no English-speaking personnel available and Lynn King is frustrated in her attempts to leave a message. Flaxo takes a message but fails to respond. These latter two companies fall by the wayside.

EARNING TRUST   What have both these companies failed to do? Communicate. In Eston's case it tried to tackle a market that it wasn't prepared for. The basic essence of communication is to talk in the same language. If you're not prepared to tackle a foreign market, due to lack of available language ability, then don't be tempted. Around the world there's indeed a prevalent use of English within business; however, you're unable to say whether or not your selected target in Germany, Russia, Chile, China or wherever has a good level of understanding English. Bring in competent personnel with a second language and then utilize their ability for maximum effect. Brief the switchboard operators on the language and advise them of the people to whom the caller should be put through.

Flaxo fell down because it didn't respond to the message that was left. There may be a number of reasons for this. It may be that the message wasn't received by the appropriate person or that it was put to one side due to a heavy workload at that time. A decision may have been taken not to pursue Sabig, as its requirements aren't really in line with Flaxo's capabilities. Whatever the reason, the fact remains that it didn't respond and this has besmirched the good name of Flaxo. Don't encourage buyers to talk you and your company down by providing them with the opportunity. Anyway, should Flaxo not have followed up the quotation, rather than wait to be contacted?

The meeting with Sabig is centred around the technical input required on these particular parts. This includes the right choice of material and the design of the product to facilitate ease of manufacture, including tool size, and negate the need for secondary processes. A number of suggestions and ideas were discussed with each company and a clearer understanding of their technical capabilities is gained by Lynn King. The four companies met with Lynn King and a design engineer from Sabig. Despite its enthusiasm, Cresta was dropped from further involvement as it had limited technical expertise and did not have the necessary computer-aid design (CAD) facilities.

If you're the salesman at Cresta, what have you failed to do? Firstly, you didn't anticipate the need for CAD; you're in a meeting to discuss design and should've recognized that there'd have been such a need. You may be a small company with limited resources but in order to satisfy companies, such as Sabig, you should form a relationship with an outside engineering design company or consultant. This also enables you to counter the second reason that you were dropped from being able to develop this opportunity further: limited technical expertise. Having the technical back-up of an outside company/consultant provides your company with a cost-efficient solution for technical support as and when required, rather than committing your limited financial resources to a technical department that would be under-utilized.

Of the remaining three companies each is asked to requote based on a small number of technical changes that Sabig's design engineer has implemented. The key to these meetings is to find out exactly what points the buyer wants to discuss. You are then able to attend the meeting fully prepared and with the right personnel.

○ *The quotation is in on time, but the buyer has a query and contacts you and ask the question. You should respond as quickly as possible to show enthusiasm and efficiency.*

○ *As other questions are raised be aware that many of these may have come from someone other than the buyer. The purchasing manager or an engineer may have asked for clarification. If you respond quickly, the buyer can respond quickly. This makes him or her look good amongst colleagues.*

○ *The buyer has worked efficiently and responded quickly, so now begins to both trust and respect you. You're helping the buyer to do his or her job well.*

THE REQUOTE

Sabig has announced a small number of technical changes, so each company will have to requote based on these changes and, unless drastic changes have been made, the new prices will be expected to be lower than the initial prices.

Even without technical changes, the purpose of the requote is often to drive the price down further. As previously mentioned, some companies will issue a target which takes into consideration the lowest quote that they received. Some buyers will ask for a requote, knowing full well that the potential suppliers will sharpen their pencils and trim the prices to even more competitive levels.

The difficulty with requotes is knowing how much to sharpen your pencil by. It may be better to reply that the prices that you supplied were your lowest possible. Alternatively, you may opt to advise that your prices will fall by 3 per cent per annum over the next 4 years as a result of your company's increasing efficiency in producing the part in question. Whatever you decide, reply within the time specified by the buyer and, if you requote, be able to justify to the buyer the lower price. Often it's worthwhile checking the specification of the product to ensure that all your costs are correct. If you need to sharpen your pencil, then your costs have to be more precise to ensure that the part will still be profitable for you to make.

At some stage in the process you should ensure that the buyer is actually comparing like for like. Companies, quoting to Sabig, have had to estimate weights, which led to Lynn King breaking all prices down on a price per gram basis. It may be that your product has different features than those your competitors or that your costs are based on using different machinery.

THE PLANT VISIT

On receipt of the requotes Sabig opted to visit Beta and Readon The latter was financially strong and its level of investment in new plant, equipment and technology was impressive. It had a good export record and demonstrated a high competence in producing and maintaining quality. Readon was starting to introduce cell manufacturing techniques and develop quick mould-changing methods to reduce the amount of time that the machines were inoperative. When initially quoting, it had also impressed Sabig by suggesting that the logo should be integrated with the moulding, rather than being pad printed. This measure would reduce the part costs as there would be no requirement for printing process and materials. Another benefit was that the appearance of the product would not deteriorate due to excessive handling and from being maintained in a damp environment, i.e. the bathroom.

Beta, which has had its fair share of problems recently with Sabig, was able to demonstrate a number of measures that it had implemented to ensure that there would be no future shortfalls in deliveries. The SQA engineer was more than satisfied with all the new procedures that were being implemented. Beta was keen also to display its recent investment programme, with new equipment recently purchased. There was a clear understanding of Sabig's requirements and the communication between the two companies had always been good.

Initial plant visits will generally see the buyer together with an SQA engineer, or other technical person should the SQA engineer not be available to make the visit. Their purpose is to ascertain the true ability of the company and gain a greater understanding of the company's approach. Management and employees, as well as processes, will be under scrutiny.

EARNING TRUST

Again, it's important to be prepared for such visits. Let the staff know who is visiting and why. Stress the importance of the visit and ensure that everything is clean, tidy and in order. Cast a critical eye over all aspects of the company. Look for strengths to be highlighted and ensure counter measures are prepared for any weaknesses that the visitors may highlight. Welcome the visitors and allow them open access to your plant, have a presentation prepared and ensure plenty of time for questions and answers.

PRODUCT DEVELOPMENT

Sabig knows that it requires an injection-moulded plastic component; knows the shape and size of the component and has already specified the type of plastic that should be used. After further consultations, there were a number of decisions taken that included a slight design alteration that would not affect the performance of the part but would give a 5 per cent reduction in the volume of material required and, therefore, a 5 per cent saving on the material costs. A different material was also proposed that had similar properties to the original material specified. There was no saving on the cost price but process times would be better as the new material was easier to mould. With these new specifications in place a further quote was required.

In many instances there's a need to provide technical input to finalise the design of a product before committing it to manufacture. Product development periods vary considerably and depend upon many factors. Different industries often have different ideas on how long the product development cycle should be. Obviously, the complexity of a product affects the cycle as does the variety of material options. There'll be a deadline involved and it's worth investing the time and energy to impress a new buyer with your skill and competence. It's worth identifying, early on, if prototype parts will be required, and the costs of producing parts should be discussed and agreed sooner rather than later.

WATCH OUT!

In some instances, buyers have exploited a supplier's technical ability, and when all the specifications have been finalized, they've requested quotes from a number of suppliers. Though this isn't a regular occurrence, in a situation where you're dealing with a potential new buyer it's important that communication is maintained at all levels of the company. Purchasing, engineering and quality should all be contacted and kept informed of the various issues. In developing a relationship with more than one department you are continually strengthening your chances of developing the business. Your technical input is then recognized at several levels within the organization and it's harder then for an individual to become exploitive of your input.

Shortly after the visit to your plant, Sabig announces it's entering into an agreement with a distributor in the Far East. This is the first time Sabig's shaving products will be launched in that region, and it's expecting a large upsurge in product demand. Immediately on reading this in the *Financial Times* you think that there may be better volumes to be had in the near future with Sabig. In your eagerness you contact Lynn King. She apologizes but says that she's currently involved on another project and will be unable to make any further decisions for some time. You feel as though she's putting you off. The reality is that she has to ensure that her existing suppliers will be able to cope with the new increased requirements. She has to secure information on the current mould tools to see if new tools will be required to facilitate this increased demand.

Two weeks later, having got over your feeling of dejection, you decide to phone again. Initially she's in a meeting but you catch her later that day. She explains the situation and advises you to phone again in two weeks. You put a note in your diary.

WATCH OUT!

○ *Delays are almost inevitable within the buying process. Projects get pushed to one side whilst day-to-day problems are resolved. People go on holiday and without their presence no further decisions are taken.*

○ *Companies run as lean operations see personnel pulled in all directions. Don't be put off by delays. How many times have you procrastinated, hesitated and changed your mind? Companies are only human.*

the order

Lynn King and the SQA engineer of Sabig meet the purchasing manager and product development manager to discuss the visits to Beta and Readon and then to discuss Asholt's merits.

The conclusion was that Beta, though implementing a number of new procedures to rectify past problems, was also introducing new equipment and that there'll be a learning curve before it reaches an acceptable level of performance. Rather than give Beta further business, which may compound the problem, the decision was taken not to give them the order.

The argument for Asholt was very strong as it had supported Sabig through good delivery/quality performance and through its technical expertise. It was well known to Sabig and familiar with the demands and requirements. Lynn King would've been quite happy to give this order to Asholt but it didn't have a cost-cutting culture and showed little initiative in proposing improvements. From her personal point of view, taking on a new supplier meant additional work and some additional, though hidden, costs. However, she had a target to hit on reducing costs and so argued that you, Readon, should be given the order. The SQA engineer also felt that it would be prudent to have another cost-competitive source for plastic mouldings as there was still a question mark over the performance of Beta.

Subsequently, the order was placed with your company, Readon. You'd initiated cost-saving ideas and were technically very able. Despite being based overseas, you'd demonstrated good communication skills throughout the process, which had negated any fears about distance. From your records you'd shown a good export delivery performance coupled with a good-quality performance. You were competitive and the recent introduction of cell manufacturing techniques and quick mould-change methods would increase your efficiency. This would facilitate cost-cutting exercises and drive down further the costs to Sabig.

WATCH OUT!

○ *When appointing new suppliers there are hidden costs that both the buyer and you must consider. There are the extra administration costs, new EDI transactions, more delivery requirements, more technical input required, more quality assessment required and increased demand for supplier development activity.*

○ *Generally, for both parties a new supplier and/or new supply contract mean extra work in the buyer monitoring and providing a service to the supplier and in the supplier, providing not only a product that's easily accounted for in the selling price, but also a service and attention that will be required to maintain the buyer/supplier relationship.*

**THE TOOLING
ORDER**

In this instance the initial order that you received was for tooling. The terms were for one-third to be invoiced on receipt of order, one-third to be invoiced on the supply of samples and one-third to be invoiced upon approval of samples. A small number of adjustments were made and the material types and colours agreed upon before approved drawings were issued for you to proceed with.

The importance of tooling costs varies amongst different manufacturing processes. Hence, payment terms will also vary, and in some cases may be non-existent. Some buyers are insisting that they'll pay no tooling costs and that the onus is on the supplier to cover its own tooling costs. This can be covered by amortization of the tooling, which increases the piece price and then makes your piece price uncompetitive. This is a vicious circle, which, in areas where tooling costs are high, is probably best avoided by not targeting companies that operate such policies. Often tooling cost terms can be settled along the lines of one-third payment with order, one-third payment upon supply of initial samples and a final payment after the supply of production parts commences.

INITIAL SAMPLES

Sabig received samples before the deadline which were labelled, as per its request, with tags that it supplied. There was some dimension discrepancy on some of the parts. As you'd arranged for each cavity to be numbered, it was easy to identify which cavity was causing the problem. The cavity was amended and a second batch of samples was approved. These initial samples were used for prototype builds, though it had been deemed unnecessary to produce prototype tools.

WATCH OUT!

○ *Deadlines should always be met. With samples this is the first opportunity that you've had to actually deliver products to the buyer. Samples that arrive late don't get the supply relationship off to a good start.*

○ *Many companies operate a procedure for the issuing of initial samples, and it's important that through your communication you're fully aware of the procedure.*

the follow-up

For the initial samples, the quality control function at Sabig has acted as expediter, to ensure that the samples were delivered as requested. The expediting on production orders is then maintained by Lynn King, to ensure that products are delivered as and when required.

TIMING AND SCHEDULES

Sabig is introducing EDI into its scheduling and purchasing system, though the majority of its suppliers get orders and schedules by fax. You receive the first production schedules, that show six weeks ahead the planned requirements. Sabig then plans its production accordingly to meet these requirements.

Many large companies now operate EDI systems to issue schedules to suppliers. As technology advances we'll soon reach a point where all companies will be expected to have EDI and all schedules, and eventually invoicing, will be handled by computers.

Even the most organized and professional of companies have problems at some point with schedules. Some schedules are so erratic that they demand the utmost flexibility from the supplier. Buyers don't like erratic schedules as it's a weakness that doesn't help them negotiate price reductions. Suppliers don't like erratic schedules as they interfere with the smooth running of the company and can have a serious knock-on effect.

You may feel that the solution to avoid difficulties is to build up a supply of parts that can help fill those times of peak demand. This may well work where the schedules go up and down but have a certain predictability. There's also cost implications in maintaining a level of stock and this has to be accounted for.

○ *Sticking to dates on quotations and deliveries is one aspect of earning a buyer's trust. Another area is honesty.*

○ *If there are problems in meeting schedules, put your hands up and admit the problem. Trying to cover problems only compounds them. They become unmanageable, you forget what you claimed in your last conversation so you go on to repeat yourself and it's brought to your attention. Now you have to fast-talk your way out of that one.*

○ *Honesty earns respect and trust.*

delivery

You deliver the first production components on time and within the right packaging. Your company must now work on maintaining a good level of service, which will enable you to build your business with Sabig.

PACKAGING
To facilitate delivery in the lots as required by Sabig's production line, a form of packaging was agreed that was efficient for both parties' use.

Packaging within any market sector where products are manufactured is an add-on cost. As with all costs this should be also treated as an area that can save time and money for both parties. Re-useable packaging has only to be purchased once, it doesn't have to be replaced, but the economies of returning empty packaging have to be considered. Whatever packaging is used, you may be able to utilize the buying power of a large customer to secure cheaper packaging.

4

buyers' expectations and power

By knowing what buyers expect and where their power stems from, you can plan ahead your strategy and approach knowing you will meet their demands and strengths head on. You can make a relationship with even a powerful buyer work for you.

introduction

This chapter aims to identify the expectations of buyers, and how they utilize your desire to meet these expectations, to gain the upper hand.

buyers' expectations

Through an appreciation of the buying function, process and buyers' powers we can begin to formulate the expectations of the buyer and tailor our company to meet those demands. It's no use trying to sell your products if the marketplace demands cannot be met. For example:

- an electronics company may decide to develop a car alarm for fleet users without being able to supply any technical back-up

- a consultancy may opt to develop business within personnel selection without the necessary experience.

These examples reflect a lack of understanding of the buyer's expectations. So how much work do we need to do to gain an understanding of their expectations?

In fact the work is a continual process that's being carried out via all your other activities, such as sales visits, market research, product/service supply and account management. All your company's activities are a source of information that provides you with the knowledge of what the buyer expects from you. Without this pool of knowledge your sales and marketing campaign will soon flounder. Your approach will be based on what *you* think should be heard and not on what *the buyer* actually wants to hear. Buyers' expectations are important, and products, services, brochures, advertising and media campaigns should be tailored to those expectations.

THE DANGER You have a salesman who visits a key account twice a month. The sales reports make interesting reading and business is good. Since opening the account there have been several discussions concerning your company's lack of EDI facilities. Any reference to EDI has now disappeared from your salesman's visit reports. Eight weeks later you lose the account.

Failure to recognize the needs of buyers happens all too often. We hear their expectations and view them as some unattainable ideal and, whilst we lay stagnant, our competitors nip in and meet all the demands. Technological, cost, logistical and many other types of demands are placed upon us. Yes, there must be some form of priority, but ignore their demands at your peril. In the above example, the salesman had got so bored with listening to the buyer's rhetoric, that he became deaf to the demands. It was a side issue that had been aired within your company and then disappeared, when other issues came along. The salesman should have made more noise about the lack of EDI facilities, and the management should have taken the buyer's comments seriously.

WATCH OUT!

○ *If a buyer expects something to happen then make sure it happens. If you lose an account because of your company's failure to meet certain demands, then that account will be ten times harder to re-open than it was to open the account initially.*

○ *If the expectation is unreasonable or will take some time to meet, then communicate this to the buyer.*

GOOD LISTENING AND GOOD REPORTING

Too many sales and marketing personnel spend time looking for hidden agendas and meanings, trying to read between the lines. Part of the art of good listening is being prepared to question issues and points, to collate the information you desire. If in doubt, ask. Buyers would rather you have a direct understanding of their expectations, rather than trying to formulate your own ideas, based on what *you think* the buyer meant rather than what the buyer *actually* meant.

So, what are buyers' expectations? They'll vary from one sector to the next but broadly speaking they'll cover such issues as costs, logistics, quality, technical/design capability and future developments.

SUPPLY PERFORMANCE – 'WHAT WE WANT, WHEN WE WANT IT'

Buyers don't allow you to dictate delivery terms. They have their own schedules to maintain and won't allow you to interfere with that. Now nobody expects miracles, but beware of the buyer who looks for impossible delivery schedules, merely to use them as a negotiating point. You specify a lead time of six weeks and the buyer wants it in two. Depending on the product or service being provided this may not be unreasonable, but you should know what is and isn't reasonable. Have lead times shown a reduction within your industrial sector? Are the buyers' expectations being affected by your competitors' performance? If so, why can you not compete?

Your company's supply performance will be assessed continually. It's no good in this day and age getting one delivery wrong out of every three. The capital equipment supplier may think that, as it supplies a one-off product, supply performance doesn't have a continual effect on it. What about the demands for technical support, advice and spares, etc.? These are all elements which go to making a good supply performance.

A buyer may specify just-in-time deliveries, which takes us back to 'What we want, when we want it.' There's no difference. Buyers want your products/service to meet their needs. They may want the component to be delivered in line with their assembly operations, or they may want the recruitment consultancy to complete its search for a new marketing manager to coincide with the introduction of a new marketing strategy.

Buyers' supply requirements aren't what they think of and then specify. They come from within their organizations. The supply requirement could originate from marketing – see Figure 4.1 below.

Figure 4.1

Marketing originated supply requirements
Marketing department **successful marketing campaign**
puts pressure on
Delivery department **to deliver more goods**
puts pressure on
Production department **to make more goods**
puts pressure on
Goods-in **to acquire more stock**
puts pressure on
Purchasing department **to buy more stock**
puts pressure on
suppliers to meet increased demand

Here we have a successful marketing campaign that has resulted in more demands on the delivery department to ship increased volumes to its customers. This in turn has led to an increase in the demand for products from the production department, which has in turn requested more goods from the goods-in department, to enable production to increase its volumes. Goods-in requests futher products from purchasing, which then requests higher volumes of goods from you the supplier.

FAST TRACK

Look at your own function and demands. You may well have had a similar effect on your company's purchasing department, which has in turn led to difficult supply performance demands from your suppliers.

You are being assessed

Whatever product/service you supply is assessed on your total performance. This incorporates such elements as supplying on time, using the correct documentation/format, speed with which queries are dealt with and quality of products/service. The buyer may or may not have a structured assessment process for grading of suppliers, either way be assured that you are being continually assessed.

ERRATIC SCHEDULES

The demands that the buyer has to place on you are often hampered by erratic scheduling. This makes it all the more harder for you to plan your production and deliveries effectively. Your resources become stretched and what was once a profitable account can become loss-making. Unfortunately, these losses are not immediately visible. Even more unfortunate is that in our haste to satisfy the difficult demands of buyers, we're setting a precedent that allows them to continually get away with issuing erratic schedules.

Your supply performance and the grading of your company is affected by the scheduling that you receive and your ability to perform to those schedules. If you struggle and perform badly you're in danger of being downgraded. This may put your company in the spotlight for the wrong reasons. Eventually, a competitor is brought in and slowly you begin to see your volumes drop. This enables you to perform better, as you're handling smaller volumes but, regrettably, just as things seemed to be improving, the buyer switches 100 per cent to the new supplier.

If a company is displaying signs of erratic scheduling, work with buyers to identify from where this stems. The schedules being issued may be usual for them, probably because no one has advised them otherwise. They may have adopted an attitude that all suppliers, within your field, are generally incapable of delivering as required. This has created an aura of general adversity between buyers and suppliers.

The buyer as consultant

So often, in the manufacturing industry, you hear of a buyer and his or her company that provide a service to their suppliers that highlights the suppliers' inefficiencies and helps to establish world class manufacturing techniques. In essence, this consists of pointing out your faults and areas for improvement, then working with you to overcome the faults and implement the changes for improvement. No supplier responds negatively to genuine assistance and neither will a buyer and his or her company respond negatively to ways in which they can improve their performance.

When faced with erratic schedules contact the buyer and understand where and how these schedules are put together. Put together a report that highlights how the scheduling ties in directly with your production and the effect that it has. The buyer wants you to be a world class manufacturer, working from an efficient cost base. Problems that buyers are creating need to be brought to their attention. They will appreciate how these problems affect your cost base, but only if you illustrate it to them in one form or another.

FAST TRACK

Don't tolerate erratic scheduling. Highlight the problem and work with the buyer to ensure that you can continue to supply quality products within the delivered time frame. If you continue to lose money, due to the buyer's poor performance, be brave enough to drop the account and advise the buyer why you are doing so.

QUALITY

A consistent quality performance isn't always easy, but it's necessary and is what the buyer expects. Poor quality is soon discovered and noted. The reverberations of supplying a shoddy product are felt throughout the buyer's company. The way you respond to quality concerns is critical, as the buyer will expect a rapid response. Failure to do so will be highlighted as your company's lack of genuine interest in the quality concerns of the buyer's company.

You may have a number of trade-specific and general quality accreditations which the buyer would expect to see. Your performance in total quality to meet the needs of the buyer is what the buyer now wants to see clearly demonstrated. He or she expects to see all quality criteria met and any quality concerns are to be dealt with immediately. Remember that quality is an issue that covers your company's total function. It isn't only about the quality of product that you supply, but also about the quality of the total service that you provide. As such, the buyer will therefore expect a total quality service. The way your receptionist answers the phone, the way your salesman conducts himself in meetings and the liaison between your technical personnel and the buyer's technical personnel are all aspects where quality is an issue.

To fulfil buyers' expectations make sure that your company has a strong quality philosophy that's instilled in the mind of all the employees. That's where quality begins, and without that support you'll fail to meet the expectations of the buyer.

It's all in the mind   Just as you educate your staff to think quality, you should also educate your staff to think marketing. They should be aware that everything they do at work relates to the marketing function of your company. Companies that collectively think marketing will strive to satisfy the needs of the buyer. A thorough understanding of the effect each person can have on the marketing function allows them to become more buyer-oriented.

price and costs

The old adversarial buyers were only concerned with price. They would have certain expectations of what is and what isn't a good price. Today buyers expect a competitive price but also want to know where it came from. For this they need to know the costs that make up your price. This again will increase the number of expectations that they will have.

Companies within the same industrial sector will be expected to have similar costings for labour, processing, raw materials, overheads and profits, etc. Major deviations within one company's costings will tell to the buyer that the company in question has no real understanding of its cost basis and, therefore, is unable to justify any of its pricing. A company that has no control or understanding of its costs is one that will go nowhere fast. These costs are expected to be revealed at the buyer's request and are normally revealed in the format of quotation support documentation. Once your competitors reveal their cost structure you'll be forced to do the same.

tooling

One of the aspects of the business-to-business market that often has to be considered is the need for tooling. Tooling costs and how they relate to your business are essential for you to understand. Buyers expect you to be familiar with tooling and in particular how it affects cost.

Tooling means different things to different people, depending upon the industry sector in which you work. In essence, tooling is an add-on piece of equipment that mates to your existing plant and machinery and allows you to produce the required component to the required shape. Tooling could be a mould for plastic mouldings that allows plastic components to be moulded to the required shape when the tool is fitted to a plastic moulding machine. It could be a metal pressing die, which fits to a metal pressing machine and allows the metal to be pressed into the required shape. Tooling could be a jig to hand bend metal pipes to a specified shape. It could be the cutting implements that are set on a turning machine to produce turned parts in the shape required.

The importance of tooling to the sales and marketing function varies considerably between industries, and the greater the importance to your industry the greater your need to understand the tooling function.

Within the manufacturing industry the need for various types of tooling, such as moulds and dies, adds a further dimension to the selling process. The cost implications for both the manufacturer and the buyer of the tooling varies from product to product. Tooling for turned parts is substantially cheaper than tooling for castings; tooling for plastic mouldings is higher than tooling for pipe manipulation.

Tooling for new projects

For new projects, most companies will cover tooling costs as part of the capital costs set aside for the new project. Indeed, if that company is then passing the tooling cost on, to another company, it will often add a margin for itself within the tooling charge. As we've seen in previous chapters, that your involvement at the design stage of a new project is of increasing importance, and increasingly expected, the toolmakers input into the development of the product can also have a significant bearing on the costs. They may make a suggestion that allows the tool to function more efficiently and, therefore, more cost effectively. It may be that they propose a tool design that can negate the need for any secondary operations, such as the trimming of a moulded component.

Some companies are moving towards the supplier paying for the tooling. In return, the supplier is being guaranteed supply for the lifetime of that product. Depending upon your own company's product and the associated tooling costs, this type of proposition may or may not be attractive. Either way it's worthwhile ensuring that you're the sole supplier, on either a global or local basis. Be wary of products that may have a long life span but are likely to undergo a number of changes during their time. This could involve you in expensive tooling upgrades which are difficult to budget for. This raises a further point in tooling amortization: always allow for a certain amount of tooling refurbishment costs, as should the tool begin to show signs of wear and tear, the customer will undoubtedly point out that it's *your* tool. Avoid cheap tooling because you're footing the bill, as the refurbishment costs will be expensive and negate any saving with which the cheap tooling may have originally provided you.

Tooling for existing projects

The capital costs on existing projects have already been covered and any additional capital investments are only likely to be made where the piece price is significantly lower than the current price, unless the existing tool requires replacement or refurbishment.

This investment in new tooling also has to be considered against the expected life of the product. The buyer has to asses the benefit of the new piece price and look at the overall saving that can be made for the life of the product. This 'payback' will give a clear indication of the point where the tooling costs will be paid for and the true piece price saving begins. The following is a simple example.

	Existing supplier	Potential new supplier
Piece price	£1.00	£0.90
Annual volume	100,000	100,000
Annual costs	£100,000	£90,000
Life of product	4 years	4 years
Tooling costs	nil	£10,000

From the above we can identify a potential saving of £10,000 per annum, which equates to £40,000 in total for the life of the product. If we deduct the tooling costs we see a total saving of £30,000.

Initially this looks very attractive; however, the buyer also has to take into consideration the return that he or she would get if the £10,000 was maintained in the bank for four years. There is also the re-sourcing costs that must be considered, such as quality audits, setting up new procedures for the new supplier and the monitoring of the new supplier's performance, which is always more intense with a new supplier than with an existing supplier on an existing product. All this extra activity costs money and could easily cost in the region of £20,000, making the initial saving of £30,000 now equate to £10,000 over the four years.

Where the piece price is lower than the existing price, there's the possibility of amortization, which may still give a competitive piece price but obviously requires an initial investment from your company.

The return on your investment has to be carefully considered and the security of the supply contract ensured.

In the above example the tooling costs could be proportioned over the four-year period though it would be necessary to calculate the return on the capital employed (ROCE). However, amortizing tools over this kind of period can present a number of problems. Volumes may drop, any problems that result in a new alternative or second supplier being introduced will affect volumes and your ROCE, and the buying company may go into liquidation. Therefore, it's general practice to amortize tools for much shorter periods, say 12 months but no longer than 24 months.

In the above example again, if we assume a ROCE of 5 per cent, then the £10,000 capital outlay at the end of one year would give a return of £10,500. With an anticipated volume of 100,000 the new price would be:

$$\frac{£10,500}{100,000} \quad + \quad £0.90 \quad = \quad £1.005$$

This price would be for the first 12 months and reduce to £0.90 for the remaining 3 years.

From the buyer's point of view the ROCE on the £500 extra that they would have to spend in year 1 is significantly lower and less of a consideration than the £10,000 which they would have to invest in a new tool. Instead of having to spend £10,000 the buyer can now look at the ROCE, on this money, over a four year period. If the buyer uses 5% as the ROCE, then a gain in excess of £2000 will be achieved. Therefore, over the 4 year period, the potential new supplier can offer a saving of over £11,500. This is well below the immediate perceived saving of £30,000.

The overall savings can be boosted further by considering the ROCE on the piece price savings to be made in years 2, 3 and 4.

With amortizing costs on existing items, both parties are taking a risk and each individual company has to decide whether or not to amortize based on the merits of each case. It's important to have some form of verification of volumes and life span of the product. Only with precise figures can you successfully calculate the costs of amortization. In this age of open-book policies don't be afraid to ask buyers to verify volumes. They will understand the need to ensure that your investment is sound.

Transfer of tooling Tools are transferred where supply, on an existing component, switches from one company to another. It's common where companies retrieve tools from suppliers that have gone into liquidation but less common where tools are required to take advantage of a lower piece price.

The cost of transferring tooling has to be carefully considered by the buying company as there are a number of elements to be considered. The tool may not be compatible with the new supplier's plant and equipment. Stocks will have to be built up to allow the new supplier to fit and commission the tool, submit samples for approval and to begin supply. For a company involved in lean manufacturing, the increase in stock level from three days' supply to three months isn't an attractive cost proposition. There may not be the space available, and outside warehousing may have to be purchased. The tool may require refurbishment due to wear and tear or poor tool maintenance.

Tooling margin Many suppliers will add some margin on the tooling costs, particularly where tooling costs are generally high. Though not a hard and fast rule, generally where tooling costs are high so are the tool maintenance costs and these costs have to be covered.

In today's competitive world it's necessary to ensure that any tooling margin added doesn't make the tooling costs uncompetitve and lose you the chance of gaining new business. When competing against a company that has shown a lower tooling price, as long as it doesn't produce its own tooling, you should be able to compete by either decreasing your tooling margin or by improving your sourcing for tools. No company should lose potential business due to tooling costs, unless of course you are a toolmaker!

Sometimes companies will view tooling margin as compensating for having to trim margins on the piece price. Be aware that in a climate of year on year cost reduction pressures the piece price targets may be impossible to reach. Trimming margins on the piece price and recouping profit on the tooling can, therefore, sometimes lead to future difficulties and is best avoided.

Where your're a second- or third-tier supplier you can be sure, particularly on new projects, that your tooling costs are being passed on with, possibly, a further margin being added. Alternatively, they may be amortizing the tooling costs. It's worth being aware of how the buyer treats your tooling costs. Costs that are being passed on won't be as critical as high tooling costs that need to be amortized.

Tooling payment terms

On high-cost tools, the payments are an area that may require negotiation. The buying company won't want to part with the full tooling cost at an early stage' and a normal compromise would be for costs to be made one-third with tooling order, one-third with the delivery of samples and the one-third being made upon approval of samples. Many buyers automatically operate a system along these lines.

In-house tool making

Where tools are relatively simple and easy to make, then toolmaking in-house presents few problems. The more complex, more expensive tools will generally require a well-equipped tool shop. Having your own tool shop is a benefit as it puts you in control of tooling costs and expands the capability of your company. To recoup capital expenditure on setting up an in-house operation, it's important that buyers realize that this facility has to be a profit centre in its own right. They expect the tooling to be competitive, but you should avoid being tempted to provide tooling at cost. This may gain business, but the piece price will also need to be competitive and it would be wrong to assume that the margin, in the piece price, will cover the investment required for the tooling operation. The capital costs to set up your own in-house tool shop will vary considerably between process types. You should, however, be at least geared up to carry out basic tool maintenance.

WATCH OUT!

Know if your competitors produce their own tooling or not as they will have greater control and flexibility over price.

TOOLMAKERS

Those industries where tooling technicalities and expense are high are supported by a network of independent toolmakers. Some specialize in specific areas such as press tools or moulds, while others will cover most types of tool requirements, though these may further specialize in developing tools for large or small components. Either way, know your toolmaker.

As the marketer you may believe that the toolmaker is the responsibility of the technical/engineering/design department and shouldn't necessarily involve you. What happens if the tool is delivered late? Who has to contact the customer to advise it that you cannot deliver the parts on time? *You* do.

Reputable toolmakers that deliver a quality product on time help you to do your job. Customers like to be kept informed of events, and being able to advise them that the tool has arrived, as scheduled, is the first sign of the professionalism of your company. This is obviously of particular importance for that all-important new customer.

Toolmakers that offer a good price but fail to deliver, as scheduled, reflect upon your company. Ensure you're basing your quotes on a reputable toolmaker's figures. Don't be afraid to develop your own relationship with your main toolmaker. It can provide advice and offer solutions to problems that your own engineers may not have thought of. This isn't because your own engineers are inadequate but because the toolmaker is a specialist in its field. Its perspective can often help in identifying more beneficial tooling configurations or ways in which the part could be altered to produce a lower-cost tool. A quick phone call to the toolmaker could mean the difference between gaining or losing a contract.

To test whether you know and have faith in your toolmaker, ask yourself if you would be happy to bring any of your key accounts on a joint visit to the toolmaker. The answer should be yes. The standards that it's working to should match or exceed yours. If they're lower, you'll always struggle to supply the quality product that you so desire. A toolmaker in which you've every confidence can liaise directly with your client to get immediate answers to any questions that may arise. This displays a strong working partnership with your toolmaker and enhances your reputation as a company that works in partnership with, not only its customers, but also with its suppliers.

TOOLING CONFIGURATIONS

Tooling is advancing all the time and this book doesn't cover these advancements and the technicalities. However, an appreciation of tooling configurations and the effect that they can have on you and your company is of importance. The first rule of tooling configurations is that they must be compatible with your own machinery. For example, a plastic moulding company that's looking at a 4-cavity mould which will produce a 1kg component from each cavity is wasting its time if, say, its machines go up to a locking force of 125 tonnes, as the machines would be too small. The converse is the moulder with machines that start at 125 tonnes where the requirement is for four 1g parts from a 4-cavity tool. Sure, the mould might fit but this would be uneconomical in the extreme.

When you weigh up the tool configuration all the factors have to be considered, such as volume per annum, life of the part, size of machine that would be required and the capacity it would take up. Mixed-cavity tools, i.e. those that produce different components from the same tool, can often be more economical, but be aware of different demands for components run from the same tool. Running one type of component from the tool has a detrimental effect on the margin within that part. Calculate the break-even point, e.g. a two-cavity tool will run with only one part being produced, instead of two, for 20 per cent of the time. Your price would be based on this ratio. However, depending upon your margin, there would be some scope to produce only one part for, say, 35 per cent of the time before production runs start to operate at a loss. Be honest with buyers and advise them of this break-even point. By working with them you should be able to ensure that the break-even point isn't breached.

Prototype/soft tooling

On low runs, soft tooling that is generally made from aluminium alloy, which, being a softer material, is easier for the toolmaker to work with and is therefore cheaper, will often be used. Due to the soft nature of the tool it's not an alternative to steel for long runs, as it won't be able to withstand the wear and tear of producing components in high volumes.

This type of tool also, in single cavity configurations, lends itself to the production of prototype parts. The speed with which the material can be worked on is quicker than for steel, and samples can be produced for the customer within a matter of weeks. The ability and willingness to become involved in such projects helps to enhance your company's reputation with the customer.

buyer power

In business-to-business marketing, the power of the organization's buyers lies essentially in a number of background factors, which are determined long before you pick up the phone to call them. The dilemma is that the buyers have what we want but we *might* only have what they want. This immediately gives buyers the upper hand – they know you want to sell them a product and/or service. They have at their control a series of weapons that can be utilized at the appropriate times. These are all hurdles for you to struggle over, barriers to be blown out of the way.

This chapter takes a cynical look at the buyer's arsenal. It tells us what we're up against in the war and allows us to prepare ourselves for the battles that lie ahead. There's never just one way to win a battle. The winning is a part of the overall strategy that's discussed in chapter five.

Which weapons buyers use vary from company to company, industry to industry, though the key elements are:

- better market knowledge, generally harnessed from you and your competitors
- often they are bigger organizations
- the market share
- the proportion of your capacity that the buyer's company takes
- the knowledge of your company's own plans to increase capacity
- the utilization of economies of scale
- a team buying approach
- the use of preferred supplier lists and vendor rating systems
- the product's life cycle
- the complexity of their product
- the uniqueness of their product
- the global sourcing policy
- the usage of quotation support documentation
- the supplier reduction policies.

MARKET KNOWLEDGE

Where do buyers get all that knowledge from? They must spend hours reading trade journals. In fact they get it from the one place that's the most difficult place for you to get it from – your competitors.

'Believe it or not, I know more about the business that you're in than you do.'

Believe it. That buyer has probably seen more manufacturers and suppliers of your product than you have heard of. They have shared many of their intimate secrets with the buyer, who has gained insights into the industry from all of them. This education cannot be rivalled for its level of information as no amount of researching through company returns, trade magazines will match the intimacy of the knowledge that the buyer receives.

This knowledge can help buyers to focus on key issues which need addressing to satisfy their demands. It can then be used to focus on your weaknesses. In doing this buyers are continually weakening your position and making you amenable to concessions.

SIZE

Often companies within the business-to-business market, end up negotiating and supplying products and services to companies that are much larger than their own. The recruitment consultancy to Pepsi, the steering systems manufacturer to Volkswagen, the computer mice to IBM are all examples of a supplier smaller than the buyer.

'We are bigger than you, so we can be twice as arrogant.'

You have heard it said before that size is not everything. Maybe not, but it sure makes some people arrogant. The fact is that when companies are large, their purchasing power is strong because we all like to have their volume business to drive our companies forward. So we all fight for those big volumes whilst the fat cat licks its lips and squeezes us dry.

Buyers will stand back and watch the fight, knowing full well that they'll indeed have achieved their goal of low-cost product. Some may say that this flies in the face of partnership sourcing and the ideal of a win-win scenario. Though buyers have the upper hand, it's the marketers that start the fight. The professional buyer will remain aloof from the fray and stick to his or her agenda of partnership sourcing and the win-win scenario.

MARKET SHARE We all like to supply market leaders, those at the forefront of their industries and markets. This increases the competition, for which buyers are grateful as they can easily identify several sources and the competitiveness between the suppliers is self-perpetuating.

> *'With our ever-increasing market share we believe that your prices should be reduced.'*

You are locked into this company. It's going from strength to strength and in return for that, if you want to maintain the business, it'll quite happily ask for a cost reduction and expect to get it. Your dilemma is that you don't wish to lose substantial business and so you must enter negotiations on price from a weak position.

THE PROPORTION OF YOUR CAPACITY THAT THE BUYER'S COMPANY TAKES Whether they take a large or small proportion of your total capacity, buyers can work this to their advantage.

> *'We take so much of your production, that whatever we ask for, we know you will agree to.'*

Yes, the buyer appears to have been your best friend in recent years. The amount of business he or she has put your way has stopped you from developing too much other business because you've been so busy. Turnover has trebled in two years. The buyer is so dependent upon you that this is a relationship that's made to last.

But then it's payback time. Recession, increased competition, greed, whatever it is, it suddenly hits you. They're looking for a 10 per cent price reduction on all the products that you supply. It cannot be done, it's not possible. But what are the consequences if you don't agree? The business is placed elsewhere, possibly a little at a time. Before you know it volumes are plummeting, you're making staff redundant, you cancel your holiday and begin panic marketing.

So the alternative is to agree to the buyer's 10 per cent cut and try to increase your efficiency and reduce your costs. The buyer's company may try to assist in this efficiency drive and initiate a number of cost-saving ideas. Then it turns round and asks for the full benefit of these cost-saving ideas, that it initiated, to be passed on to the company. Instead of assisting you to reduce your own costs for your benefit and to help you achieve the target of a 10 per cent cut, what the buyer has done is to get you to agree to a 10 per cent cut and then identified areas where additional savings can be made, for the buyer's benefit.

'We know that we only take a small proportion of your total capacity, but we also know, that you know, that our overall spend in this area is more than 20 times what you supply us.'

Of course the buyer knows that you know. He or she made a point of telling you. If you have one foot in the door, with the potential of significantly increasing your business with the buyer, then you'll fight to keep that foot in the door. You're open to make concessions, to enable you to build and develop the business. Your presence is good for the buyer because it keeps the current suppliers, who take the large proportion of the buyer's requirement, alert to the requests of the buyer.

KNOWLEDGE OF YOUR COMPANY'S OWN PLANS TO INCREASE CAPACITY

You're about to invest in a new machine. The buyer knows it as you've told him with pride of your company's investment. There's an opportunity for the buyer to secure capacity from you at a reduced rate. It's unlikely that new equipment and machinery are fully utilized from the start. The buyer knows that you would prefer some return for your investment even if it's not as much as expected.

'I hear you have two spare pages available on next week's magazine. We could make use of that for you, though at a heavily reduced rate of course.'

You invest in capacity to meet anticipated market demands. Then that market lets you down. You're left with spare capacity. Enter the buyer. He or she knows that you would prefer to use that machine or fill those pages rather than let the opportunity go to waste. It makes economic sense to get some financial return for your spare capacity. So don't be surprised when the buyer makes you an offer.

UTILISATION OF ECONOMIES OF SCALE

By centralizing a company's or organization's needs buyers have more purchasing power. Instead of buying a small percentage of the total requirements for any particular part they now buys 100 per cent. This is the same 100 per cent share that you want, and the question that the buyer asks is to what price are you prepared to go to acquire some, if not all, of this 100 per cent.

'We have centralized purchasing and now the amount of your product that I buy has increased tenfold, and as a current supplier you're well placed to gain more business. Incidentally, have I told you our aim is to decrease the price tenfold?'

One minute you're in a strong position to gain more business, next minute you're ready to pack your bags and go home. To make matters worse the other 12 manufacturing bases of this company will introduce even more competitors to the negotiating table, all of whom will be 'well placed to gain more business'. If each operation has two suppliers for your product and you already share the business with another supplier then your immediate competition will rise from one to twenty-four.

Buyers will build your hopes up for the business that you may attain under economies of scale. The volumes look attractive and this enables you to provide very competitive pricing. This is what the buyer wants – companies bidding against one another, for a dramatic increase in their volumes, and, probably, against a selection of non-current suppliers. Prices reduce dramatically and the buyer can pick and choose the supplier. However, the buyer chooses three suppliers and what you thought was the original volume you quoted on, is now only a one-third share. All your careful calculations and predictions are wrong, but this still represents a large amount of business. You take the one-third share but don't risk blowing it all by increasing the price.

TEAM-BUYING APPROACH

Increasingly, companies have the buyers working with a number of other personnel from key departments such as engineering, quality assurance, marketing, planning and production. Before they can make a final decision to buy they are often working to make the decision as a team with the other personnel.

> *'I am meeting my purchasing manager to discuss all the quotes and then I have to meet with engineering, production and quality assurance. Then I'll speak to my purchasing manager again before speaking to marketing, then back to quality assurance, then over to.........'*

These meetings could involve anyone and everyone. The type of market, and from where the need stems, will generally dictate those personnel who attend these meetings. This is where buyer power becomes team power. Have you ever noticed that it's easier to talk to someone on a one-to-one basis than it is to talk to a group of, say, 10 people? Have you ever noticed how difficult it is to talk to those 10 when they're all in different places? For every objection that a buyer may raise somebody else will raise another. In team buying several objections can arise, continually putting you on the spot. This continual barrage of objections weakens you and opens the door for the buyer to ask for concessions.

In such circumstances, the decision is taken by a general consensus from those within the meeting. To ensure a good representation at the meeting, you establish contact with several key personnel of the buyer's company and when they meet they'll all know of your company. Instead of one or two people looking at how you could make concessions in order to reduce costs, you have a whole team. Ideas fly round the table and three days later you get a report that says in essence that you can have the business but … and reels off three pages of concessions that they would like you to make.

USE OF PREFERRED SUPPLIER LISTS AND VENDOR RATING SYSTEMS

Many buyers operate both a preferred suppliers list and a vendor rating system. The concept of preferred suppliers immediately implies that it's very difficult for new suppliers to become involved. However, it also implies that for existing suppliers to remain existing suppliers they must maintain their presence on this list through meeting the concessions requested. The vendor rating system is generally the first step to secure a listing as a new supplier and is the first step, for an existing supplier, to demotion from the list.

'We have a preferred supplier list, but we do buy in excess of $5 million of your product type.'

For the potential supplier this is generally followed by 'Keep in touch'. Buyers shut the door and then invite you to pursue them. They know you cannot ignore business of that proportion. They know you'll keep in touch and will gleefully grab any opportunity to quote or prove your worth. This teasing keeps you at arm's length, until the time is right for them to ask you to quote. Then when you quote, after being teased along for so long, they know that you won't be prepared to let it go easily and will do your utmost to secure the business. This increases the competitive pressures and drives the price downwards.

For the existing supplier there's the possibility of increasing your share of that $5 million worth of business. Buyers want to remind you so that you'll play ball when it comes around to discussing prices. You may be a preferred supplier but you know you aren't the only supplier. So you fight your corner of the business and hope to come through as a winner and increase your share. You have security and threat all rolled into one.

> *'We have a very tough vendor rating policy which only a few suppliers, like the 5000 we already have, can meet.'*

Buyers like to think that their vendor rating system is different and indeed some of them might have slight differences. However, if you already supply a similar sized company, within that sector, it's unlikely that there'll be any drastic differences. Buyers want to be in control. They'll vet suppliers and ensure that all requirements are met. They'll continually adopt and develop new and demanding vendor assessment criteria, along with their SQA allies, which will put pressure on you to conform to a number of criteria. Fail to meet these criteria and it could cost you the business. It may cost you money to meet these criteria but these cannot be reflected in your costs to them. You may be competitive but your competitors may operate better quality systems; it may even be that the buyers' new criteria have arisen from a visit to a competitor. You have to implement changes and meet the new criteria or lose the business.

Meeting these criteria is so often a prerequisite to dealing with many companies and in doing so you're raising the stakes and pushing further forward the expectations of the buyer. This in turn enables the buyer to apply further pressure on you, and in your weakened state don't be surprised when a request is received for a 3 per cent price reduction.

> *'We are reducing the number of suppliers.'*

This provides buyers with two sources of power. One is the implication that if you want to secure any business with them it's going to cost you in terms of time and concessions. You'll need to argue against their policy and force them into accepting a new supplier, which is contrary to their aims. To convince them, you'll be amenable to no end of concessions but will glow with pride when you break the barrier and secure their business. And by the way how profitable is that business?

The second source of power is one yielded against the existing supplier, which must improve the quality of the product, agree to more deliveries per week, increase alterations and changes and then still look at ways of reducing costs to ensure that no one undercuts it.

GLOBAL SOURCING The immediate threat with global sourcing is that the number of competitors widens. Developing countries enter the fray and introduce new, previously unheard of low costs. In dealing with these countries there are many issues to consider, and though the more developed countries can maintain, to some degree, the upper hand the pressure on costs is notable.

'We operate a global sourcing policy.'

Hold on! This is an opportunity for a new supplier to get a foot in the door, not a source of buyer power. Yes, it's an opportunity but it's also a source of buyer power. Global sourcing immediately conjures up images of hundreds of companies all bidding for the same business. It makes the sourcing much more competitive. It says that if you want to get involved, you'd better be very competitive, otherwise you'll not stand a chance.

Global sourcing is an abused term and in some cases buyers may actually be inviting only 10 companies to quote, which is more than the two that they normally invite. They may have no intention of changing suppliers but use you to drive the price down of the current supplier. They know you'll give a good price because (a) you want the business and (b) they have made it clear to you that they operate a global sourcing policy. It's interesting to note that some suppliers have a policy of not responding to companies that say they're operating a global sourcing policy. These people must fear competition and be afraid of revealing their lack of competitive edge.

'In line with our global sourcing policy, we're going to ask the other 5,000 suppliers who haven't yet quoted for their prices to supply what you currently supply to us.'

The number of competitors in the marketplace obviously increases the competitiveness for supply. Buyers know this and will make full use of it. Don't then be amazed when the buyer turns around and tells you that he or she has had several quotes cheaper than yours.

PRODUCT LONGEVITY All products have a life span. Developments, trends and fashion will continue to push products forward. This life span, in the hands of the buyer, becomes a tool to secure a better deal.

'Our product has a very long life cycle.'

You could have good business here for a long time. The buyer knows that you would like a long stable supply contract. It enables you to plan for the future and provides you with a certain amount of security. To get that security will cost you and this enables the buyer to apply pressure to ensure that he or she gets the right price.

QUOTATION SUPPORT DOCUMENTATION

As a tool this documentation is useful to the buyer in making comparisons between quotes. It can be open to abuse by both parties and rather than use it to assist you, in your strive for competitiveness, some buyers may use it as a negotiating weapon.

'We know your cost structure and believe that your profit margins on this part are too high.'

Once you've kindly filled in the quotation support documentation, buyers will then quite happily turn around and advise you of what they think is a fair profit margin. Remember, buyers want to be in control and if they're allowed to control your finances they will.

5

getting the strategy right

Relationships that are built on the correct marketing strategy will last and develop, unlike those based on opportunistic deals. This chapter dispels a lot of the myths about marketing and strategy and provides a simple and effective way of getting the strategy right.

responding to the challenge

So how do we respond to the challenge posed by today's buyers? It's clear that business-to-business dealing is a complex process and a piece-meal approach isn't the answer. What is needed is an integrated response across all business functions and processes. This chapter tells you how to integrate your company's response to the buyers' challenge. The buyer-oriented vision which can provide this integration is marketing. The discipline which can deliver a framework for action is called business planning. The answer to the shut-out is: buyer focus combined with business planning. This chapter will also give you a clear picture of what having a buyer focus means and talk you through the entire business planning process.

implementation

The wise manager, before he or she engages in any strategic business planning exercise, will have a good, hard look around at his or her organization and colleagues, because there are a number of decisions to be made before engaging in any kind of business planning.

If the company has a planning culture, there'll be an annual cycle of analysis, synthesis, decision-making, implementation, communication, control and feedback. The manager or executive has a place in this process, a place which is determined primarily by his or her function and workgroup, but also by his or her informal networks. It's relatively easy to get a handle on this process, work out what it's really about and bring forward practical business ideas for discussion.

If there's no planning culture, however, and the company lives from hand to mouth, there's a need to question the direction the company is going in. Few organizations will survive without a game plan, a programme of action that helps reduce risk and uncertainty. In an organization with no game plan, you have to ask: is there any point in trying to work out a business plan? If you're the boss, of course there is, but if you're an employed manager or executive, who will be your allies? Will you waste a lot of time and energy trying to sell colleagues on the idea of business planning, before you even start talking about the content of the specific business plan for the company itself? Would it be better to find another company which has a clear sense of where it's going and invest your energies there?

Even in an organization with an acceptance of the constructive benefits of planning, gaining acceptance for your reading of the market, let alone your recommendations, is not automatic.

Organizations are divided into groups. The strategy planner needs to be aware of who belongs to what group, what their values and priorities are and how they behave. The next step is to work out which groups can be helpful and to build bridges to them.

Organizations tend to emphasize certain things they consider important, e.g. customer service. Nobody can argue against that. When it comes to presenting your ideas, it's helpful to piggy-back on top of one of these sacred precepts. People cannot then take shots at you without attacking a core value of the company.

People in organizations generally don't like change. Their resistance to change is caused by their work habits, personal predisposition, educational and professional training perspective, fear of the unknown and mistrust of their superiors' and colleagues' motives. All power comes from the CEO and the board. To overcome resistance and make change effective, their buy-in has to be secured. Otherwise, you're knocking your head against a brick wall.

So before doing any strategic thinking, look ahead to the implementation. Sometimes it's a good idea to put the cart before the horse. If there's no planning culture, if the levers of power are just that bit too much out of your grasp right now, if the proposal which is emerging in the back of your mind runs counter to the prevailing culture and the opposing groups may be too powerful, think again! Maybe there's another company out there which would be more receptive to bold, practical and imaginative ideas.

business planning

The business planning process is summarized in Table 5.1. Later on in this chapter, we'll look at each of the business planning steps in sequence. But firstly, it is necessary to discuss marketing and its potential for helping companies put it all together. Before we do that, it is necessary to answer the question as to what marketing actually is.

so what is marketing?

It's easier to answer this question by first of all saying what marketing isn't and also look at the bad press marketing has been getting.

MARKETING ISN'T SELLING

Saying marketing is selling is like saying a computer is a screen. Sure, a screen is a very important part of a computer, but it isn't the whole thing. Selling is a part of marketing. In fact, selling is what puts the bite into marketing. If you don't make the sale, you don't recruit or retain the customer.

The trouble is that marketing is seen as sales and associated in people's minds with used-car dealers, doorsteppers and insurance pedlars. When many people think of sales , they think of flashy smiles, high-pressure talk, arm-twisting, artificial rapport and insincerity. 'You don't like the refrigerator, ma'am? You're such a nice person, I'll tell you what I'm gonna do. I'll throw in an alarm clock. Deal?'

You may have seen the film *Groundhog Day*, in which Bill Murray plays a character who wakes up to relive the same day every day. He's trapped and cannot get out, even when he throws himself under a lorry in an effort to kill himself. Every day, he meets an insurance salesman who, apparently, was at school with him. He epitomizes the salesperson who tries to sell you something you don't need (who needs life insurance if you're not going to die?). He is full of false bonhomie and Murray's techniques for dealing with him are very instructive. Nobody likes that kind of salesperson – but that isn't marketing!

Table 5.1

The business planning process

Key process elements	Sub-elements	Description
Creative vision		» Work out the mission statement
Corporate objective/strategy		» Develop corporate objectives (e.g. ROI) » Decide the corporate strategy (e.g. organic growth, acquisition)
Take the market apart	Context	» Analyze the business environment
	Customers/Buyers	» Research buyers and their needs
	Categorize the buyers	» Work out a segmentation of the market on the basis of the buyer/prospect information
	Competitors	» Analyze the closest rivals to work out competitive positioning
	Company	» Audit your organization for marketing excellence » Do an analysis of strengths, weaknesses, opportunities and threats in each segment
	Critical success factors	» Work out the critical capabilities your organization needs to succeed
Segment		» Decide which segments to target
Marketing objectives and strategies		» Develop marketing objectives (e.g. share, share growth) » Decide whether to use market penetration, innovation, new market development or diversification
Buyer relationship framework		» Decide how the total mix of business processes is to be configured so as to build and maintain constructive relationships with buyers
	Buyer management	» Allocate resources to account management » Monitor progress against buyer-related objectives
	Buyer need	» Decide on the basis of buyer need the specification for your service/product
	Buyer cost	» Decide on a cost and price structure that delivers value for money, consistent with quality
	Buyer information and communications	» Develop an information and communication management system to exploit all prospect/buyer contacts
	Buyer convenience	» Decide how the service or product is going to be made available to the buyer for his or her convenience
	Bought quality	» Work out quality management processes which will deliver a quality product to the buyer
	Bought process	» Ensure compatibility of operations/production process with buyers' requirements

IT'S NOT ADVERTISING EITHER

Advertising is the most visible part of marketing, consequently it's what people react to or think of as marketing. This also has a bad press, because it's seen as wasteful, encouraging competition and duplication of effort. People believe advertising also lies to them in order to persuade them that something is what it isn't. And who pays for the ads anyway? Why, the customer. Unkind words like hype and bullshit spring to mind. Well, nowadays it's important that manufacturers, retailers and service providers are able to inform people about their products. That need has always existed. Let's not confuse it with the whole marketing process.

AND IT'S NOT PR

Marketing isn't PR, or media and public relations either. There's a misconception of PR as another version of the art of telling lies, a corporate tool for spreading misinformation. There's some truth in this, because companies have in the past used PR for this purpose. Marketing suffers from the association. But marketing is no more PR than it's advertising or selling. All three are sub-activities of marketing.

SOMETIMES IT CAN LOOK LIKE A RELIGION, BUT IT'S NOT

Quite a few people who make marketing their career, write books about it or teach it at business school regard it as a kind of religion. Marketers, they believe, have a mission to convert the world to right-thinking values, buyer-oriented values.

According to the marketing fundamentalist, everyone in the company should sing out of the marketing hymn book. Every thought and action of company workers should come from a love for the buyer. Marketing should dominate the actions of the corporation. The problem with this attitude is that it just creates resentment among non-marketing functions. The marketers think the marketing plan should say it all, and include all of the other functions' activities. Operations managers will prefer to call it a business plan, not a marketing plan, because in their minds, marketing is only another function, not the whole shebang.

This is all fine, except for one thing. Marketers will tell you that 'the buyer is king', but no one, not even the most fervent marketer, has ever said that 'the buyer is God'. If the buyer isn't God, then marketing cannot be a religion. (Some companies think their brand is a god, for whom they make strange sacrifices, and in whose service the workers must lose their individual identity, but that's another story. That's more about mind control than marketing.)

WELL, IS IT JUST BULLSHIT, THEN?

A lot of people outside of marketing, and even quite a few salespeople, believe that marketing is bullshit. They've worked perhaps with people in marketing who don't understand the business, who have a fundamental lack of expertise, or who are impractical – 'They don't make anything with their hands, for Pete's sake! They just talk.' At least if you sell, you talk to the buyer (and hopefully listen, too). Chances are, you might even make a sale. But marketers just talk *about* the customer. They're unproductive – and expensive.

Well, it's true. There are a lot of people in marketing who just shoot their mouths off and, just before what they like to call their 'strategy' crumbles, you find they've moved on, got promoted or landed some big job with a blue-chip company. That's life! That doesn't mean that all of marketing is nonsense!

MARKETING IS JUST A RAG-BAG OF BORROWED IDEAS WITH NO COHESION?

Again, there's some truth in this. As an academic subject, marketing grew out of economics. Nowadays, it draws on a wide range of sources for its insights: psychology, sociology, economics, anthropology, semiotics, geography and many more. Because of their subject's dubious parentage, marketing academics attract the same scepticism as their counterparts in business.

SO WHAT THE HELL *IS* MARKETING?

Marketing, fundamentally, is selling products that don't come back to people who do. It's a buyer-focused vision that can drive the organization to growth in sales and profits. The purpose of marketing, as an activity, is to recruit and retain customers – get them and keep them. Any action that helps to recruit and/or retain customers, whoever performs it, is marketing.

As someone once said: 'Marketing is too important to be left to the marketing department.' Everyone plays a part. Nowadays, in business-to-business marketing, when the operations director, quality manager, scheduler, chief executive, receptionist, financial controller, production and service operatives and drivers – not just the salesperson or marketer – come into contact with the buyer, everyone is doing the marketing.

examples of marketing

Let's look at some examples of what it is. It's marketing, if:

● an R&D engineer successfully completes the field trials of a new piece of equipment

● a cost accountant works out a price for a new radiotherapy service

● the production manager introduces statistical process control

● the salesman gets an order

● the buyer identifies two new sources of better-quality, cheaper components

● the new ad agency produces some great copy that really works

● the company defuses a local environmentalist protest by an 'open-door' policy

● the company *doesn't* cut the training, R&D and market research budgets when finances are tight

● the accounts department gets the invoicing right all the time

● the drivers always arrive within the time band at the buyer's plant

● every time the quality manager visits a client company, he or she takes a line operative to increase his or her knowledge of the buying company's requirements.

the marketing process

Given the complexity of the business-to-business buying process, there's little point in bolt-on marketing, i.e. making the product and then trying to sell it. You need to 'put it all together', that's to say, you need to integrate the operations, financial and sales/marketing groups with one buyer-focused vision.

FAST TRACK

This involves two things: thinking and doing. You need to exercise your brain in order to solve the technological and managerial problems of modern business. The answers don't always come easy or work out first time. You also need to take positive and effective action once you've done your thinking.

Thinking involves research, analysis, synthesis and decision-making. Doing things involves practical work, developing action programmes that actually deliver in practice the best fruits of your thinking.

an investment rather than a cost view of marketing

If marketers and salespeople have their faults, so have people in other functions. Since much of business is run by accountants, it becomes very cost-oriented. Every new initiative is judged by what it'll cost, which can usually be worked out quite easily, rather than by what benefits it may bring, which often aren't quantifiable with any certainty. So because a certain cost is easier to relate to conceptually, and income can be uncertain, and accountants are guided by the convention of prudence, risks don't get taken. So pervasive is this attitude that companies will spend $500,000 on some new machinery and then delay for months a simple decision about a new product brochure that costs $5,000. This is being penny wise and dollar foolish.

FAST TRACK

If a company believes in marketing, then it should invest in it. By all means count the cost, but have the guts to take an investment view. That involves risk, which is supposed to be at the core of enterprise!

mission statement, objectives and strategies

There's plenty of room for confusion in talking about mission statements, objectives and strategies. In fact, this is potentially the most confusing area of business for many people, which is a pity, because it needn't be so. The confusion is at least partly caused by the proliferation of business models and frameworks.

One of our objectives in writing this book was precisely to put the record straight on strategic thinking, to simplify it back to the essential basics. This chapter looks at objectives and strategies in some detail in an effort to do so.

levels and viewpoints

The first thing to get clear before any discussion of mission statements is an understanding of what level of organization we're talking about. It could be:

- a division of a multinational corporation

- a small one-product operation

- a large, independent company

- a corporate HQ of a multi-divisional organization.

Secondly, it's important to be clear about where the strategy formulator is coming from. What is his or her point of view? Is he or she:

- an owner-manager

- divisional manager

- group chief executive

- marketing executive

- sales director?

The corporate and marketing objectives will depend very much on the level of the organization and on the viewpoints of the person or people formulating the strategy.

the eternal triangle

All business is based on the eternal triangle: the company, the customer and the competitor. For itself, the company has corporate objectives and strategies. For its buyers, the company has marketing objectives and strategies. For its competitors, the company has competitive objectives and strategies. These are the three fundamental dimensions along which objectives and strategies are developed.

corporate mission statement

The mission statement, as we saw in chapter one, is the guiding vision of the company. It sets out the blueprint for success, a vision of the future, and marks out the organization's competitive domain and function.

WATCH OUT!

○ *Mission statements have a bad name, too. This is because often they're badly thought out, usually by committee.*

○ *Many people working in organizations know that their mission statement was thought up on the back of an envelope and stuck on the company letterhead with a new logo more as a kind of change ritual than any meaningful process. These people don't buy into the corporate vision. They weren't consulted about the core mission. They don't care, they're disenfranchised. It doesn't concern them.*

objectives and strategy

Thinking about objectives is complicated by the presence of a lot of similar words, such as targets, goals and aims. Some people try to distinguish between these words. This simply creates confusion. It's best if they're all taken to mean the same thing – what you're trying to achieve.

The same thing happens with strategy. Attempts are made to create distinctions between strategy, policy and tactics. Again, it's best if they're all taken to mean the same thing – the way you try to achieve an objective.

Objectives (or targets, goals and aims) mean what you're trying to achieve. Strategy means how you're going to achieve the objective. Strategy is how the company performs a particular activity, whether it's the result of a conscious consideration and planning process or whether it's a 'default strategy', in other words, the way things just 'happen' without anyone thinking it through.

The word 'strategic' is bandied about so much that its meaning has become devalued and now simply equates to 'very important'. Strategic marketing is simply the big marketing decisions that need to get sorted out first.

There's a possibly helpful distinction to be made between strategic marketing, which is about segmentation, targeting and positioning (see below), and operational marketing, which is about managing buyer relationships.

corporate objectives

When it comes to objectives, it's important to distinguish between corporate or organizational objectives and marketing objectives. Some people say they're the same, but in fact they're not. A publicly quoted company should regard its institutional and other investors as the primary customer targets. The corporation is competing for their capital with other quoted companies and the 'product' it provides for them is essentially the dividend. Even if a quoted company has a single product-market focus on one fairly similar type of buyer, its corporate objectives will have priority over its marketing or trading objectives.

Corporate objectives have to do with the return to shareholders from the investment in productive assets. Essentially they require decisions about what outcomes are expected in the form of profit contribution (or useful tax losses), dividends and management fees, i.e. what's the total return on investment expected.

corporate strategy

Corporate strategy is about how to achieve the desired return on investment for the shareholders or stakeholders. There are three basic kinds of corporate strategy:

- organic growth, where sales and profit growth come from the buyers in the market

- merger and acquisition growth, where the corporation buys or combines with another corporation or corporations, thereby adding huge chunks of revenue and, hopefully, profit contribution to its portfolio

- a combination of organic and acquisition/merger growth.

corporate and marketing strategies

There is an interplay between corporate and marketing objectives. There's no point setting an ROI of 25 per cent if the company's divisions are operating in product-markets where the average ROI is 10 per cent. It's simply not realistic. So the corporate objectives will always depend on the trading context(s) that underpins them. Depending on the relationship with the shareholders and the level of target return which they've come to expect, the company will seek out investments in manufacturing, service or trading operations which are calculated to give them the called-for return.

The organization can buy and sell companies until it gets the right 'mix' of investments – the right portfolio. Once it has got a company into its investment portfolio and wants to manage it for a certain expected return on investment, it has to decide how much cash to put in and the timing of the cash it can expect to take out. This is done by means of portfolio analysis.

corporate and marketing strategy in a conglomerate

If you're a company trading in a specific product-market context with a broadly homogeneous customer target, your corporate and marketing strategy will be effectively similar. However, if an organization is a conglomerate and has different divisions, each of which addresses a distinct product-market with separate and different customer targets – basically different businesses – there cannot be a single marketing strategy for that organization. Each division must have the flexibility to develop its own segmentation, targeting and positioning.

The business strategy or corporate strategy of an organization is about managing the portfolio of businesses or divisions to produce the best returns for its shareholders. The key skills in the context of a multi-divisional corporation with diverse product-markets are company acquisition and disposal, share price management and asset management.

Can the holding entity have a marketing strategy which is distinct from those of its operating divisions? Of course, but its prospects or customers are institutional and private shareholders, not the people who buy products or services from its trading divisions. It's in the equity business. Its marketing communications should therefore be focused on Wall Street or the City, on the institutions and people who buy and sell shares. From the corporate HQ perspective, the divisions are simply sources of cash, profit and management fees, which require in return sums of money for capital expenditure on productive assets.

The business strategy of a multi-divisional publicly quoted organization is multiform, because it exists in potentially three markets, which aren't directly connected to performance in the trading division markets:

- the equities market – shares of the corporation can be bought and sold any day on the exchange

- the mergers, acquisitions and disposals market – at any opportune time, it can decide to enter the mergers, acquisitions and disposals market, or it may also itself become the object of a merger, acquisition or disposal

- capital markets – it's also in the market for borrowed funds, as distinct from equity capital.

The behaviour of 'group' or 'HQ' is, therefore, dictated by the company's target customers' requirements, the pension funds, banks and analysts.

The headquarter's marketing perspective can therefore be quite different from that of its trading divisions. Clearly the needs of shareholders need to be reconciled with those of the divisions and their customers. This is a difficult balancing act. A tool for achieving that balance is portfolio analysis.

portfolio analysis

In portfolio analysis, companies are rated for how much cash they're expected to absorb from the parent or holding company. What will the investment be for the coming year in terms of capital expenditure on machinery and equipment? What will be the expenditure on labour, materials and overheads? What, then, will be the direction (positive or negative), size and timing of the net monthly or quarterly cash flow? What will be the profit yield from the cash flow?

Once the cash flow has been worked out, companies can be classified into a number of groups:

- stars – usually in high-growth markets, and requiring lots of investment, but promising big returns

- cash cows – operations which generate large positive net cash flows

- question marks – operations which require quite a bit of cash but whose future is uncertain

- dogs – business investments with poor prospects and in which the company has a weak market position.

CATEGORIZING INVESTMENTS

Decisions about which operation ranks as which kind of the above four investments are taken on the basis of:

- the attractiveness of the market

- the competitive business strength of the division in that product-market.

Attractiveness of the market is measured using five criteria:

- size

- growth

- potential profitability
- critical success factors
- intensity of competition.

As far as competitive business strength is concerned, the principal index for this is the company's market share. The bigger the share, the stronger the company. However, there are other ways of looking at this, such as a strengths and weaknesses analysis across all business functions of the operating division or a rating against the critical success factors for the business, both of course related to the competition – see chapter one, Table 1.3, for an example of this kind of analysis.

Once the corporate board has worked out in its own mind how it's going to cash-manage the investments on the basis of the realistic market position of the opeating divisions, the clear formulation of marketing objectives and strategies becomes much easier.

PORTFOLIO MANAGEMENT STRATEGIES

Once investments have been grouped in this way, decisions can then be taken about what to do with them. There are four basic options:

- *build* – invest for growth
- *hold* – defend the market position
- *harvest* – cream off the cash
- *exit* – get out of the market.

marketing objectives have a buyer focus

Marketing objectives differ from corporate objectives. They're primarily concerned with buyer relations rather than return on investment. In any company, at any time, there're always only two principal marketing objectives:

- *buyer recruitment* – to get new buyers;
- *buyer retention* – to keep the existing buyers.

These objectives have two corollaries:

- *buyer avoidance* – to avoid recruitment of unprofitable accounts;

● *buyer delisting* – to withdraw from unprofitable accounts.

The two most important objectives are buyer recruitment and buyer retention. Buyer delisting and avoidance may seem negative as objectives, but in fact they're important for a number of reasons. These reasons are discussed in the following paragraphs before we go on to talk about marketing strategy.

BUYER DELISTING   Buyer delisting is about withdrawing from accounts which in the long run won't help to meet corporate profit objectives. Each product-market context has a 'going rate' of return. You can measure your company's profit performance in any particular account against that loose norm, weigh up the benefits and costs of the relationship in the medium to longer term and decide: is it worth it? Can we continue to meet this buyer's demands without harming our company?

There's little point in continuing to service a buyer whose demands in terms of cost reduction, research and development expenditure, and process improvement aren't meaningfully compensated by growth for your company. Certainly, in many business-to-business markets, margins can be small, particularly if the company is squeezed between powerful suppliers and powerful buyers. But there's a difference between accepting a volume/margin trade-off for a written contract lasting two to three years and allowing yourself to be ripped off at both ends.

Back in chapter one, Table 1.1, we looked at a simple way of categorizing buyers – see page 21. The buyers in the low revenue, low margin category are prime candidates for delisting. In chapter six we look at partnership development, an approach to buyer relationship management which looks in detail at account revenue and profitability in the context of selecting who to work with and who to get rid of.

Despite all the preparation and research, management decisions are still taken by humans, which allows for errors of judgement to be made. The real problem arises when management is afraid to admit to failure and persists with a product, service and/or strategy that's quickly identified by its lack of acceptance by the target audience.

Three years and 6,000 names

EXAMPLE

Perhaps history's most notable example was the Ford Edsel. It was three years in development and market research had identified a potential list of some 6,000 names for the car. Against this research, the management came up with its own name, Edsel, naming the car after the son of Henry Ford, the founder. The car was an immediate failure and sold 89,000 units in two years, which was a far cry from the 200,000 per annum that was required to break even. The car had been on sale for just over two years when, in 1959, it was discontinued. The management had realized its failure and responded. The Edsel suffered a net loss of $350 million. ○

Of course, you don't do this account delisting analysis in isolation. You involve the buyer. You point out you're not making any money out of the relationship, that this is harming your company. If the buyer is smart, values you as a supply source and doesn't need the aggravation, hassle and work of going elsewhere, this will give him pause for thought. It may be he's never considered things from your side too carefully. Why should he? That's your job. If a solid business case is put to him carefully (and you've researched his options thoroughly before you do so), it could result in a change in the relationship that gives you the extra reward you need.

BUYER AVOIDANCE Calling buyer avoidance a marketing objective must be one of the dumbest things anyone ever said about doing business, right? Wrong. Do we really expect people to turn down business? Absolutely! Well, where's the next contract, the next order going to come from? Our answer is, if you've taken the market apart, done your strategic thinking and set up a framework for managing buyer relationships, you won't need to ask the question.

Boring! Howell, Henry, Chaldecott, Lury, a leading London advertising agency, which now positions itself as a '3-D marketing communications company', works with major brands, such as Tango, Mercury and Bhs. Its co-founder, Rupert Howell, is quoted in *Marketing Business* as saying: 'We turned down 60 pitches last year … 20 of them because the client was too small, 30 because we were closed to new business at the time and 10 because they were simply too boring to work with.'

Clearly a company with an outstanding success record in its field attracts a lot of work and can be selective, but it's not often that 'boring' is used as a filter to screen out and turn away business! But why not, especially if you own the business?

Robert Townsend, the former Chairman of Avis Rent-A-Car, used to ask the question: if you're not in business for fun or profit, what are you doing there? He also recommended a company should have a Vice-President in Charge of Killing Things, i.e. making sure bad ideas never got off the ground. Why not extend the principle to relationships and make sure that bad relationships never get off the ground?

SIZE

There are other reasons apart from boredom for turning away business. One is size. A smaller business may begin working with a large multiple or original equipment manufacturer. After a while, the demands for deep discounts, cost reduction, extended terms of credit, increased volumes, even crazy demands like paying for the 'privilege' of training the buying company's staff in handling your product (it happens!), become too much. You need to get out of the relationship, but it's tricky. The process of tearing the relationship apart can be painful, messy and expensive – like many divorces.

Capacity

Another reason for turning away business is capacity. At any particular point in time, the company may simply not be in a position to service an account, much as it would like to take it on. For example, a furniture manufacturer selling to retailers may normally have a delivery against order of four weeks. If there's a surge in demand, overtime working can be used to keep up. At a certain point, however, the extra labour and machine time are not enough to handle demand. The process of hiring and training new skilled operatives is too lengthy to make any short-term impact, so delivery lead times have to go out to eight, maybe ten, weeks.

In this situation, it'll be counter-productive for the salespeople to call on new accounts. In the first place, they'll be talking to buyers about a ten-week delivery, instead of four. Secondly, if they nevertheless sign up the account and start taking orders, they merely add to problems accumulating back at the factory.

The way they do business

EXAMPLE

A smaller Japanese audio electronics company was considering a manufacturing investment in Europe. The project was touted around a number of corporate finance houses to work out the least-cost funding deal. All of the banks loved the project, except one, whose business development director quizzed the Japanese closely to get an accurate picture of their marketing methods. What he heard didn't impress him one bit. His bank put in a bid to finance the project, but deliberately took a big spread, making the quote uncompetitive so as not to get the business.○

Quotations for quotations' sake

Many organizations are required by internal guidelines to request three quotations before any purchase can be evaluated. When such a company has a strong relationship with a preferred supplier, it often knows in advance what the outcome will be. The other two quotes become a formality. Quoting against such an established supplier in these circumstances is a difficult proposition. A bidder needs to work out the realistic chances of securing the business.

Don't quote me!

EXAMPLE

A printing company dealing with banking/financial services print requirements received hundreds of requests to quote per month. Its success rate was low. It never ran any analysis of which bids were successful. It had no computerized prospect/buyer database. A consultancy firm applied a simple statistical technique to a historical analysis of the quotes and was quickly able to tell the company what size of job it should focus on and what type and size it could concentrate its marketing on. This analysis was of course backed up by discussion with prospects that had and hadn't awarded contracts to the printing firm. As a result, requests to quote from certain sources could be seen for what they were, 'filler' quotes, which at that time the firm had no chance of winning because of the bigger competition. Those accounts could be back-burnered until the printer's capability had been significantly enhanced and expanded.

BUYER FOCUS   Perhaps the most important reason for turning away clients has to do with buyer focus, which means the focus on the types of buyer you have chosen to do business with. This focus is arrived at by two business processes known as segmentation and targeting, which are described below. Segmentation means cutting the market up into meaningful, manageable chunks or groups of customers. Targeting means choosing those chunks you want to go after.

So, if the organization decides it will go after medium-sized accounts, with a turnover of $3–5 million and a spend of $250,000–$1,000,000, located in a certain area and having a particular type of application for your product, that's its buyer focus, its targeting.

If, therefore, a new prospect, a small company, outside of the relevant geographic location, with a different type of application and a projected spend of $50,000, calls and wants a quote, a decision has to be taken: does the company want to do business with them? The answer should be no.

This area causes companies a lot of anguish, particularly if they're in any way panicked because of an uncertain future, or business is slack and they need orders to fill capacity. But taking an order from a company outside the target zone isn't just taking an order, it means the beginning of a new relationship. There'll be an expectation of continuity of supply, so that, when the next order comes in it's met on time, quantity and price, same as the last one. There's the issue of servicing this account with sales calls, plant visits and all the other business communications that go on, not to mention the need for changes to your operating process that may be required.

It's a matter of having faith in your buyer focus and the courage to say no, to exclude opportunity, because it's not the right kind of opportunity as you've defined it. Many companies don't have the guts for that, and so develop an opportunistic behaviour, hopping from one account to another, never really giving excellent service, just being adequate and no more. Ultimately, they're unreliable, which is the worst sin in a buyer's mind. They cannot be trusted. They're here today and gone tomorrow. Many get what they deserve – failure.

marketing strategy

Marketing strategy is about how marketing objectives are met, i.e. it's about ways of recruiting and retaining buyers. Having discussed delisting and avoidance quite extensively, we'll concentrate from now on on the two principal marketing objectives: buyer recruitment and buyer retention. There are four basic marketing strategies, or ways of achieving these two objectives:

- *market penetration* – existing offering to existing market

- *new market development* – existing offering to new market

- *process/mix innovation* – new offering to existing market

- *diversification* – new offering to new market.

the marketing objectives and strategies grid

The two key marketing objectives and four basic marketing strategies can be put together in a grid, which shows how they interrelate.

BUYER RELATIONSHIP FRAMEWORK

The buyer relationship framework is defined below. It extends beyond the traditional marketing mix and includes quality and buyer management processes.

MARKET PENETRATION STRATEGY

How does a company achieve market penetration? It can increase the number of its buyer accounts, increase their rates of consumption of the product and/or increase the total number of buying customers in the market (i.e. 'grow the market'). So, market penetration is a way of approaching buyer recruitment, namely keeping the same mix and focusing on the same type of buyer target, and either growing the market and keeping the same share, or increasing share, or both. It's also about buyer retention, because if you can increase the volume of business gained from the existing buyer accounts, that's also market penetration, growing your share of the market.

Table 5.2

Marketing objectives and strategies

Marketing objective	Marketing strategy	Market segments	Positioning/ offering	Actions and points to watch
Buyer recruitment	Existing market penetration	Existing	Existing	➢ Grow the market; take share of increase ➢ Take share of existing market from a competitor
	New market development	New	Existing	➢ Enter new market
	Innovation	Existing	New	➢ Strategy more appropriate to buyer retention; can lead to recruitment
	Diversification	New	New	➢ Double the risk!
Buyer retention	Existing market penetration	Existing	Existing	➢ Key strategy for buyer retention: increase usage of existing offering by working closely with existing buyers
	New market development	New	Existing	➢ Strategy more appropriate to buyer recruitment, but don't neglect existing buyer accounts
	Innovation	Existing	New	➢ Key strategy for buyer retention: work with existing buyers to develop new offering
	Diversification	New	New	➢ Strategy more appropriate to buyer recruitment, but don't neglect existing buyer accounts

NEW MARKET DEVELOPMENT STRATEGY

New market development is about taking the existing offering into a different market, introducing it to a new type of buyer account (e.g. a different type of application for the product) or a new region of a country, or an overseas market. Note that the word 'market' could be changed to 'segment' and the same principles would be applicable. Market development is very much about buyer recruitment, because the organization is moving into a new market or market segment.

INNOVATION STRATEGY

Innovation is about bringing a new offering to the existing market, offering the existing buyers something new. It is, therefore, a key marketing strategy for buyer retention. It means making use of the inside track your organization has with an account, your access to its engineering and quality people as well as the buyer, working the relationship productively and profitably.

Innovation can involve any aspect of the buyer relationship framework, or of the operating process. Examples include:

● an improvement in delivery from once a week to three times a week

● product modifications which give better performance benefits

● a radical new design which cuts unit variable cost in half

● introduction of new equipment which gives a more complete service

● process improvement which means less scrap and rework, and better yield

● introduction of failure mode effects analysis (FMEA), total quality management (TQM), statistical process control (SPC) or some other quality driver which assures the buyer of better process quality control

● a new pricing structure which gives buyers a better deal on certain types of order

● adoption of new means of communication, such as EDI

● involvement of the buyer's organization in field trials of a new concept or working prototype

● development of a buyer information system.

DIVERSIFICATION STRATEGY Diversification means bringing a product or service which is new to the company to a market which is also new – a process that clearly carries more risks. Diversification is similar to new market development in that it involves moving into a new market, recruiting new buyers.

combining marketing strategies

These four strategy options are not mutually exclusive. Given sufficient resources and management skills, a company could undertake initiatives in all of these areas at one time. Some organizations are in businesses that tend to require strengths in one particular area. For example, printed circuit board manufacture is one of many businesses which demand continual new product development. Innovation could therefore be said to be the dominant marketing strategy in those industries.

The four different strategies will require differing levels of resources at any given time, in any particular context. The important point is to recognize which is the essential strategy and how much it'll cost, then to build that cost into the action programme.

competitive objectives and strategy

After corporate and marketing objectives and strategies, this is the third set of objectives and strategies which needs to be taken into account. The importance in thinking about competition is not to lose the focus on the buyer. Ultimately, the buyer's needs and the ability to meet them are the determining factors. However, as the competitors are usually the most serious threat to achieving this, some hard thinking needs to be done about the competition.

The message isn't to let competitors dictate the strategy completely, but to take account of them and use your strengths to combat them. The primary focus should always be on the buyer; too much focus on the competitor is a distraction from the goal.

Competitive objectives can vary greatly. For example, at one time, Fujitsu's objective in the Japanese mainframe computer market was: 'beat IBM in Japan'. that is, to achieve bigger sales in a given year than

Big Blue in Fujitsu's domestic market. (This was achieved a long time ago!) But take, for example, an objective of increasing market share from 25 per cent to 35 per cent in one year. Is that a competitive objective or a customer-related objective? The answer is: both. It's difficult to separate the two. If the company sets a market share objective, this will inevitably translate to a competitive objective. The point is the buyer-related aspects of the objective are the key ones. Competition is secondary. This is important, because a lot of business thinking over the past 10 to 15 years has focused on competition and competitive strategy to the extent that there's a serious risk that the most important people – the buyers and prospects – get forgotten.

competitive strategies

There are four basic strategies for competing:

- low-cost leadership
- differentiation
- multi-segment
- single segment.

Low-cost leadership means having the lowest unit cost for a given level of quality – being unbeatable on cost/price. All companies should strive for this continuously, through cost control and strategic effectiveness, but there can be only one low cost leader, like for like.

Differentiation means essentially avoiding price-based competition and competing on the basis of other aspects of the buyer relationship, such as design, delivery, quality standards and product performance.

A multi-segment competitive strategy means the company has identified a number of different market segments developed a different offering for several of them and competes in all of those target segments. This type of competitive strategy requires considerable resources and is usually the hallmark of a strong company, often the market leader or nearest challenger.

A single-segment competitive strategy is where the company decides to focus on, concentrate on and specialize in, servicing a certain segment, a specific type of buyer account. Companies adopting this strategy are often smaller, highly specialized, extremely skilled and flexible operations, often doing work larger companies cannot or don't want to handle.

combining competitive strategies

These are four main kinds of competitive strategy:

- low-cost leadership in a single segment
- low-cost leadership in multiple segments
- differentiation in a single segment
- differentiation in multiple segments.

leaders, challengers, followers and nichers

It's helpful when trying to characterize your organization's competitive strategy to examine its share of the market compared to the other players. Research has shown that there are four main kinds of competitors in any market context. They are:

- leader
- challenger
- follower
- nicher.

Leader, as the name implies, means the organization with the largest share of the market in value or volume terms. Being the leader is associated with certain types of behaviour, such as being first into the market, having more customers and setting the benchmark for prices. Watching the leader, if your own organization isn't in that fortunate position, is a very useful way to set a benchmark for your own performance.

A challenger means a company which is quite close to the leader in terms of market share and in a position to make a credible challenge and become the leader. These companies often behave aggressively in terms of pricing and promotion.

A follower is a company which is a good bit off the leadership position and unlikely to mount a successful challenge. Followers tend to be content to copy the leader's practices and produce me-too products selling above the leader's prices.

A nicher is a specialist working in a small segment which requires highly specialized servicing and the volumes are too small to attract the leader.

EXAMPLE

IDA Ireland - a market leader

Conventional wisdom says that governments and government agencies are not good at providing business services. A shining contradiction and an example of a switched-on agency is IDA Ireland, the Irish government's industrial development arm.

IDA markets Ireland around the world as an investment location for organizations wishing to do business in Europe. Its objective is to contribute to Ireland's economic development through job creation and the promotion of local resource consumption. It has succeeded in attracting 1,100 overseas companies to establish key operations there.

Why should world-class companies wish to invest hundreds of millions of dollars on an island on the periphery of the European market? Well, IDA was able to offer the lowest (10 per cent) rate of corporate profits tax in Europe right up to the year 2010, highly educated English-speaking workers, cash grants against capital, training and R&D expenditure, duty-free access to the EC, a first class digital telecommunications system, a proven return on investment three times as high as anywhere else in Europe, no local equity obligation and tax-free repatriation of profits.

In the 1970s it targeted high-growth industries such as electronics and pharmaceuticals, automotive components and high-tech engineering. Since then, major hardware, test equipment and component providers, such as DEC, Wang, Prime Computer, Amdahl, Fujitsu, Dell, Gateway and Intel, to name but a few, have queued up to establish facilities there.

With the advent of the PC and the shift in power from hardware to software producers, however, there was a need for a change in targeting strategy. IDA was empowered to offer its top-flight package of cash and tax incentives to manufacturers, but the emerging growth was beginning to come in service businesses, led by computer software. IDA didn't have a product to offer. The solution, however, was breathtakingly simple: the government passed an enabling law which deemed certain service businesses, including systems and applications software development, to be eligible for the incentives package. This put IDA ahead of the field in the rush to secure the European software operations of major US corporations, and it didn't waste any time. In 1984, Lotus was the first software company to invest. Over the past 10 years it has been followed by 70 other companies, including 5 of the world's top 10 independent software houses. Names of investors include: Microsoft, Lotus, Symantec, Motorola, Retix, Ericsson, Oracle, Ask, Boole and Babbage, Claris, Corel, DEC, EDS, GEISCo, Hitachi, Hoskyns, IBM, Informix, Kao Corporation, McGraw Hill, Measurex, Norsk Data, Novell, Quark, WordStar, Fukutake Publishing, Sun Microsystems and Westinghouse Canada. There are now 4,500 people working in these companies, a testament to IDA's ability to be first to market with a new product, target an emerging growth sector and play to its strengths.

Even better news from Ireland's point of view is that the opportunities created for overseas companies were also seized by 300 indigenous software companies, creating another 4,500 jobs, making a total of 9,000 people at work in Ireland's software industry. The fact that Ireland can 'grow its own' software developers is good news for the long term.

IDA, in partnership with Telecom Eireann, the Irish telecommunications network provider, is now extending the services concept in an effort to attract central reservation centres, consumer service centres, telemarketing, direct response handling, lead generation, marketing research and technical support services to Ireland. ○

the organisation's competitive strategy

FITTING
COMPETITIVE
OBJECTIVES AND
STRATEGIES TO
CORPORATE AND
MARKETING
OBJECTIVES AND
STRATEGIES

The organization's competitive strategy shouldn't be worked out until a full segmentation, targeting and positioning analysis has been carried out. This is discussed on page 162. Meanwhile Table 5.3 illustrates how, for example, a challenger, Sydanex, might succinctly formulate its corporate, marketing and competitive objectives and strategies for becoming leader ahead of the current leader, Champion.

Table 5.3

Sydanex: challenging for market leadership			
Dimension	*Corporate*	*Marketing*	*Competitive*
Objectives	Return on investment Earnings per share	Customer recruitment Increase share	Bigger market share than Champion
Strategies	Organic growth	Market penetration	Differentiation Multi-segment

CRITICAL
SUCCESS
FACTORS

At this stage, the critical success factors identified when taking the market apart should be re-examined and the comparative analysis carried out in Table 1.3 used to feed into the SWOT analysis below.

marketing SWOT analysis

A SWOT (strengths, weaknesses, opportunities and threats) analysis is, first and foremost, a process which identifies the strengths and weaknesses, opportunities and threats of the organization.

Opportunities and threats are external to the company and appear in the environment. The strengths and weaknesses are internal and can be built up from a number of different processes:

- a functional audit of the firm, including a marketing audit

- a measurement of the firm against the critical success factors

- benchmarking of key processes against competitors or other companies in other industries

- an appraisal of the firm against the buyer relationship management framework.

A SWOT analysis is also the name given to a diagram summarizing the outcome of the analytical process – see the example below.

SAMPLE SWOT ANALYSIS

(Putting it all together)

Opportunities	Threats
New markets, segments, territories, targets, buyers Political: change of government Technology: trend is for use of company's technology Environmental: new legislation favours company's product Social: well-educated labour force available	Competitors: winning increased share Economic: recession Technology: rapid change Environmental: energy use
Weaknesses	Strengths
Poor labour relations Excessive gearing Tardy deliveries Unclear customer focus Absence of quality programme	Most profitable in industry Market share leader 95 per cent distribution coverage Clear competitive positioning

Strategy

○ *Remember that opportunities are external to the firm.*

○ *They should be seen in terms of either buyer opportunities or opportunities arising from changes in the environment.*

The reason for stressing customer opportunities is twofold. First of all, the marketer's focus should always be on the buyer. Secondly, buyers' changing needs are the primary and enduring source of genuine opportunity.

People frequently make a mistake of classifying as an opportunity a possible future company action, such as new product development. For example, the marketer sees a change in customer needs, realizes the company doesn't yet have a product to match it, so inserts new product development or new service development in the opportunity square. This isn't a correct use of the SWOT diagram. The correct place for a possible or proposed initiative by the organization is the marketing programme, which is discussed in chapter six – Managing buyer relationships'. The tendency to put company initiatives in the opportunity box is a symptom of self-orientation rather than buyer-orientation! This applies whether the initiative is a new ad campaign, purchase of new equipment or acquiring a new company.

THREATS

Environmental threats can often seem nebulous. In a disassembled array, they can seem innocuous. Their potency can seem questionable. But if you then think through how your competitors (the very real threats) may be positioned to take advantage of the adverse environmental changes, the force of the threat can be brought home more quickly.

For example, some years ago, the application of electronic point-of-sale equipment was limited. It was an emerging technology. However, one day, one of the food multiples decided to 'go for it'. This totally changed the face of retailing and gave the retailers hugely increased control over their customer information and their suppliers, altering the balance of power vis-à-vis suppliers considerably in their favour.

The change in technology in the hands of a competitor increases their power. (Buyers are competitors, too!)

STRENGTHS AND WEAKNESSES These are internal to the company. A mistake people commonly make is to look at the organization in isolation and not to realize that strengths and weaknesses are meaningful only when assessed relative to (a) buyer needs and (b) competitor strengths and weaknesses. There's little point in putting down something as a strength if a competitor possesses the same capability, only stronger.

Strengths and weaknesses need not be only in the marketing function. They can exist in any function. There are a number of ways to assess strengths and weaknesses:

● against critical success factors

● by function

● using the buyer relationship framework.

marketing priorities

Arising from the SWOT are a number of marketing priorities or key marketing issues. These boil down to:

● using your strength to take advantage of opportunities

● remedying your weaknesses to cope with threats.

strategic marketing

There's often confusion between marketing strategy and strategic marketing. We've seen four different kinds of marketing strategy above. Strategic marketing, however, includes three important processes, which are known as segmentation, targeting and positioning. These are about about:

● breaking the market into chunks

● picking the chunks to go after

- creating a unique concept or perspective on your product/service offering in the minds of the customers.

What's the point of all of this? Well, if business-to-business marketing is about meeting buyers' needs, the more clearly those needs can be broken down and understood the better. The point about categorizing types of buyer account is that this is a recognition of differences between buyers. Understanding these differences is the beginning of good buyer relationship management.

segmentation

If a buyer tells a salesperson that the product or service he or she is offering is no different from anyone else's, that'll produce a swift reaction and a long explanation of why the product is different, better, bigger, faster and so on.

Buyers are the same. If you tell a buyer his or her company is just the same as a competitor, you'll very quickly be put right. Buyers feel they are different and expect to be treated differently, and made to feel special, or distinctive. That's what segmentation is about.

WHAT SEGMENTATION MEANS

Segmentation means 'cutting'. The business thinker works out the best way to 'cut' the market. For example, a company could decide to segment the market on the basis of size of account – large, medium and small. Or it could decide that the most meaningful way to segment existing accounts and prospects would be by product application, or frequency of use.

The idea is to come up with a division of the market 'cake' into segments (sub-markets) on the basis of a segmentation variable – some feature or collection of distinguishing attributes which make a particular grouping of buyers or prospects significantly different from other groupings. An important issue is whether the segmentation variable is robust enough to support a marketing effort. In other words: does it matter enough? Segmentation, therefore, is simply a way of categorizing buyers.

Another way to look at it is not so much cutting the market into manageable-sized chunks, but of grouping individual buyers with similar needs or characteristics.

The benefits of segmentation are:

- it is easier to plan for groups of buyer accounts than for every individual buyer

- cost-effectiveness in the promotional budget is more likely

- buyers' needs are more clearly identified

- the marketing offer becomes more tightly specified, giving greater cost-effectiveness

- resources can be concentrated in high-return segments

- competitors who don't use segmentation can be disadvantaged

- because segmentation requires a careful study of buying organizations, very often this process, together with appropriate targeting and positioning, uncovers opportunities; in this sense, segmentation is the key to opportunity.

Many companies, in business-to-business markets as well as consumer markets, don't use segmentation. If this means they treat all of their customers the same, don't recognize that some groups of them have similar needs and can be accessed with a specific package tailored to their needs, then inevitably, eventually, other things being equal, those companies will lose out. Nowadays segmentation is not a luxury, it's a must.

**IS SEGMENTATION
SOME KIND OF
MAGIC?**

Some people have the idea that segmentation is a kind of magic, a black art which no one can understand. In fact anyone who's done the work of taking the market apart can simply test for viable segments, using the checklist below, which is based on the experience of many companies in many different markets.

The segmentation process is an attempt to come up with a reading of the market and of the buyers, which is more accurate than your previous one, or indeed your competitors' analyses.

How do you know your reading is the right one? The answer is you may not find out until the end of the year! Segmentation involves risk. You're betting on your reading of the market. There's no 'right way' to segment. There are many right ways to segment at any given time; some are more right than others, i.e. bring better business results. So how does someone know a better segmentation decision from a poorer one? The answer is suck it and see, trial and error and learning from experience; it comes down to really knowing and understanding your buyers and their organizations – being able to read them better than they can themselves, if possible!

Some marketers like to make out that there's a certain mystique to their art. In this, they're no different to any other profession. Segmentation can be a subtle process – after all you are trying to spot a new angle on the market, to come up with a way of looking at the market that your competitors have never tried. To that extent it does make demands on creativity. This in itself is no great problem. Often creativity is just a question of getting the right people around the same table with an excellent set of data. After that, the decision on how to segment, or indeed target or position will often make itself.

TESTS OF A VIABLE SEGMENT These are as follows:

- there needs to be a feature which distinguishes that segment or group of prospects from others

- there must be some indications that the segment prospects will respond favourably to a specific adapted offer

- the segment must have a certain adequate size

- the segment should be accessible to marketing communications

- the company must be in the ballpark.

SEGMENTATION CHECKLIST Some examples of variables or distinguishing characteristics on which business-to-business markets can be segmented or categorized are:

- benefits sought

- the 80/20 rule (the top 20 per cent of existing buyer accounts make up 80 per cent of sales revenue or margin, so find prospects like the top 20 per cent) ·

- industry type

- type of product application

- location (domestic, overseas)

- technological process used

- sourcing policy (single, dual, multiple)

- level of usage (light, medium, heavy)

- size of company (very small, small, medium, large, very large)

- buying decision approach.

BUYING DECISION APPROACH Research by Michele Bunn of the State University of New York at Buffalo has produced a categorization of organizations' approaches to the buying decision as follows:

- casual

- routine low priority

- simple modified rebuy

- judgemental new task

- complex modified rebuy

- strategic new task.

There are two principal ways in which these approaches to or types of buying decision can be broken down: by situation and by associated buyer activities.

There are four key situational variables:

- the importance of the purchase to the organization

- the level of uncertainty surrounding the purchase

- the number of options available to the buyer

- the buyer's power in the situation

In addition, buyers' activities when deciding on a buy can be broken down into four main categories::

- search for information

- use of analytical techniques, e.g. quantitative techniques

- consideration of strategic objectives and long-term needs

- reference to policies, procedures and previous transactions.

Bunn's research, published in the *Journal of Marketing* (January 1993, Volume 57, pp. 38–56) combined the buying decision approaches, situational descriptions and buying activities in one table (see Table 5.4).

Table 5.4 shows for each kind of buying decision how the buyers view it and react. Segmentation on this basis could be a very effective way to isolate key account categories, target which ones to focus on and aim communications and selling activities at them.

THE NEED FOR INFORMATION

The more information available for the business planning process, and particularly for the segmentation analysis, the better. Notice, we said information, not data. It's OK to be an info junkie, but data addicts are bad news!

Segmentation is unlikely to work if the company doesn't have a thorough information system which regularly delivers a stream of top class information on prospects, customers and competitors to board and executive levels across all aspects of the operation.

BEING IN THE BALLPARK

Segmentation should be done taking into account what the organization can actually offer. When a separate segment is identified, a check must be run on whether the company's current offering can meet its requirements. Is the company able to compete in this particular segment – is it in the ballpark? Any gap must be covered by an action plan, if that segment is to be targeted in the future. The action plan will include any capital expenditure necessary to give the organization the capability to compete in that segment and also an operating budget for developing and marketing the new mix.

Table 5.4

Descriptions of buying decision approaches

Variables	1 Casual	2 Routine low priority	3 Simple modified rebuy	4 Judgmental new task	5 Complex modified rebuy	6 Strategic new task
Situational characteristics						
Purchase importance	Of minor importance	Somewhat important	Quite important	Quite important	Quite important	Extremely important
Task uncertainty	Little uncertainty	Moderately uncertain	Little uncertainty	Great amount of uncertainty	Little uncertainty	Moderately uncertain
Extensiveness of choice set	Much choice	Much choice	Narrow set of choices	Narrow set of choices	Much choice	Narrow set of choices
Buyer power	Little or no power	Moderate power	Moderate power	Moderate power	Strong power position	Strong power position
Buying activities						
Search for information	No search made	Little effort at searching	Moderate amount of search	Moderate amount of search	High level of search	High level of search
Use of analysis techniques	No analysis performed	Moderate level of analysis	Moderate level of analysis	Moderate level of analysis	Great deal of analysis	Great deal of analysis
Pro-active focus	No attention to pro-active issues	Superficial consideration of pro-active focus	High level of pro-active focus	Moderate pro-active focus	High level of pro-active focus	Pro-active issues dominate purchase
Procedural control	Simply transmit the order	Follow standard procedures	Follow standard procedures	Little reliance on established procedures	Follow standard procedures	Little reliance on established procudures

○ *Segmentation is never done on the basis of the organization's own product or service. That is a product-oriented rather than a customer-oriented view which can lead to mistakes.*

○ *Buyers' needs should always be the focus.*

○ *Differentiate the product, but segment the market!*

○ *Remember! Segments have legs! This means that segments are groups, but groups made up of individual buyers.*

targeting

Targeting takes place once the segments have been identified. Targeting simply means selecting which segments to go after, focus on, specialize in, concentrate on or stick to.

Isn't it better to go after them all? Well, for one thing, it costs a lot of money to go after them all because the idea of segmentation is that the segments are so distinct that they each need a separate offering to be developed for them. Secondly, what happens if you succeed in them all? Can you handle it without the risk of overtrading?

There are five criteria for assessing the attractiveness of a segment and its suitability for targeting:

● level of competition in the segment

● potential profitability

● size of segment

● growth of the segment

● potential responsiveness to a specially adapted offering.

WAYS OF TARGETING

There are basically four different ways to target (i.e. types of targeting strategy):

● multi-segment (also known as differentiated) targeting – the organization selects a wider range of segments to chase. A separate, distinctive buyer relationship mix must be developed for each one

- single-segment (also known as concentrated, or focused) targeting – the organization picks one segment and targets it alone. This is effectively specialization, or niche targeting, equivalent to a single-segment competitive strategy

- undifferentiated targeting – this is basically where there is effectively no segmentation, and no account is taken of potential differences between customers or their needs. The company offers the same mix to every prospect

- custom targeting – this involves treating each different prospect as a separate segment with unique and distinct needs. Such a strategy might be appropriate to manufacturing organizations selling complex products into a small number of major buyers, or indeed to consultancies, where each new account needs to be taken separately.

TARGETING A SEGMENT EFFECTIVELY SELECTS THE COMPETITION

The alert reader will have spotted a connection between targeting strategy and competitive strategy. Let's look at it again.

Competitive strategies	Targeting strategies
Multi-segment Single-segment	Multi-segment Single-segment

In other words, the single-/multi-segment choice is common to both. The reason for this is that the number of segments a company targets defines not only the breadth of buyer needs it will service, but also, clearly, the scope of the competition it'll face.

Where there are buyers, there are competitors. When you choose your target buyers, you automatically choose the competition as well, like it or not!

positioning

What is positioning? Behind this whole concept, one of the most important in marketing, are a number of ideas:

- each company, product or service occupies a position in the mind of the prospect or buyer

- this position is a quasi-unconscious representation of the company, product or service by the buyer

- the position can be represented in a diagram (normally two-dimensional, but it can be multi-dimensional)

- competing companies and their products, services or brands can also be allocated a space on this diagram, so that the original company's position relative to customer need and the company's competitors scope can be worked out.

- Some people talk about 'competitive positioning', as if position vis-à-vis the competition is the key. However, it's the position vis-à-vis the buyer which really matters. The choice of segments to go after, in other words the targeting, will determine who the buyers are and, therefore, who the competitors are. Competitors follow buyers, so the people who matter for positioning purposes are the buyers, not the competitors. Below is an example of a positioning diagram or chart (also called a perceptual map, i.e. a map of the buyers' perceptions). Using the price and delivery axes, the position of the three competitors can be plotted. According to buyer perceptions, A is best in terms of price and delivery. The competitive advantage of A can be read off the two axes.

POSITIONING AND BUYER RELATIONSHIP MANAGEMENT

In order to work out the positioning of a product or service, it's necessary to identify its sustainable competitive advantage and the benefits which make it different from the competitors. This is best done with the aid of good marketing research. Research can also help identify the need to reposition the existing product or service and therefore acts as a useful guide to marketing strategy.

Positioning has to do with position in the buyer's or prospect's mind, nowhere else. Every prospect has an ideal position of what he or she wants to purchase. This can be explicitly stated or may be latent or unconscious. Buyers receive lots of information and messages every day. They screen out what isn't essential. In order to be heard above the din and to get through, to actually communicate with them, it helps to have worked out a unique positioning. If this can be translated into a catchy slogan or strapline, there can be big payoffs. A simple example of a positioning statement contained in a slogan is Unipart's '*Yes*ability'. This conveys a positive attitude and capability, and asserts reassuring, trust-building characteristics in the buyer's mind.

Figure 5.1

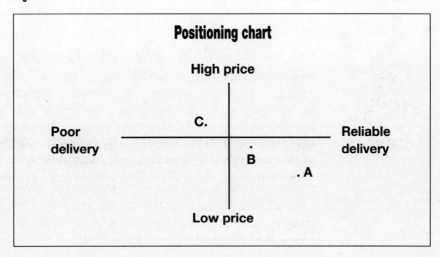

○ The image you are trying to position in the prospect's or buyer's mind should be credible, consistent and clear.

○ A product's positioning is the informing image that guides the working out of buyer relationship management.

○ Positioning is essentially the same thing as 'image'. Consequently, it's not surprising that there's a close link between positioning and buyer communications. Buyer communications, supported by the other elements in the buyer relationship management framework, is the primary method by which positioning can be created and maintained. This is examined further in chapter six.

○ We've advocated in this chapter a buyer focus and clear business thinking and planning as two key ways of striking back at buyer power. Not only is it necessary to understand the market trends better than buyers, it's essential to think smarter than them as well. Paradoxically, buyers must form the central preoccupation of the selling effort and everything must be done to earn their trust and to construct a mutually profitable relationship.

○ It's important to keep the eternal triangle of company, customer and competitor in mind and to understand the differences between and the relative importance of corporate, marketing and competitive objectives and strategies.

○ The two key marketing objectives are buyer recruitment and buyer retention. At the same time, avoiding or terminating certain accounts can also be good business decisions. The four main marketing strategies are market penetration, new market development, innovation and diversification.

There was also a discussion of competitive strategies, single- or multi-segment, low-cost or differentiation.

We then considered the major marketing activities of segmentation, targeting and positioning. This process highlighted the benefits of segmenting buyers, selecting the most desirable accounts and creating a unique image in the mind of the prospects in those accounts.

It was emphasized that the important position is that which the company, product, service or brand occupies in the buyer's or prospect's mind. The creation of this unique position should be informed also by competitive differentiation, but is ultimately characterized by the distinct or unique benefit which the company or its product offers.

next chapter

Following the business planning process gives the marketer/salesperson an essential framework for the next and final chapter. In it we discuss buyer relationship management. In other words, the strategic thinking and planning has been done, and we now go on to look at practical methods of recruiting and retaining buyers.

6

managing buyer relationships

Having taken the market apart, thoroughly grasped the buyer's function, process and expectations and worked out the right strategy, you still need a framework for managing relationships with buyers. This can be achieved by using the seven-point framework contained in this chapter.

introduction

Having considered corporate, marketing and competitive objectives and strategies, the company should now be in a position to look at the ongoing management of buyer relationships.

the buyer relationship framework

To manage buyer relationships, it's helpful to have a framework, which we call the buyer relationship management framework (see Table 6.1). This is the set of internal activities or variables the company can control (as distinct from the environmental or external factors which it cannot control) in its work of initiating, reviewing, constructing, developing, improving, renewing and terminating relationships with buyers.

Traditionally, the marketing mix was made up of the 'four Ps': product, price, place and promotion. This framework is no longer adequate to handle today's process- and quality-oriented relationship management in business-to-business markets.

Recasting the marketing mix to make it more buyer-oriented and adding three more elements, the buyer relationship framework mix looks like this:

Buyer relationship framework	Old marketing mix (Four Ps)
Buyer management	——
Buyer need	Product
Buyer cost	Price
Buyer information and communications	Promotion
Buyer convenience	Place
Bought quality	——
Bought process	——

Table 6.1

The buyer relationship mix and marketing strategies

Buyer management Mix elements	Dominant marketing strategy Existing market penetration	New market development	Process/mix innovation	Diversification
Buyer management	Focus resources on existing accounts	Focus resources on new accounts	Innovation is developed mostly for existing accounts, but use innovations to attact new accounts	Focus resources on new accounts and innovation
Buyer need	Maintain existing product or service	Some adaptation of product may be necessary for new market	Meet buyers' needs with a new product, service or mix	Meet new prospects' needs with an innovative development approach
Buyer cost	Seek continuous cost reduction	Offer the new prospects an attractive total acquisition cost	Make sure the innovation contains cost advantages for existing buyers	Offer the new prospects the innovative mix at an attractive total acquisition cost
Buyer information and communications	Deepen the quality of information on existing accounts. Encourage increased usage and repeat business. Finetune the positioning.	Research the new market. Develop a new communications mix. Market-test the positioning.	Create early awareness of the innovation. Sell the new benefits to existing buyers. Check fit with existing brand values.	Create awareness in the new market. Stimulate trial purchases.
Buyer convenience	Improve logistical support to existing buyers. Reduce lead-times.	Check out logistics issues in new market segments. Adjust accordingly.	See what contribution logistics can make to the innovation.	Check out logistics issues in new market and assess potential for major contribution.
Bought quality	Continuously review quality drivers and performance in existing accounts.	Make sure company meets quality criteria of new market prospects.	Use quality drivers to inform the innovation process.	Make sure new mix meets quality of new market.
Bought process	Continuously improve operational capability on existing accounts.	Check the acceptability of the operational process to the prospects in the new market.	Make sure process innovation goes hand in hand with product or service innovation.	Check the fit between the new mix and prospects and the new operations process.

Here is a brief explanation of the framework elements:

● buyer management has to do with the management of buyer accounts, resource allocation, and feedback and control

● buyer need has to do with the managing of the fulfilment of buyers' needs with products and services

● buyer cost deals with pricing from the point of view of cost to the buyer

● buyer information and communications involves all communication and contact with the buyer and the management of information generated about buyer accounts

● buyer convenience has to do with making the product or service physically available to buyers in such a way as is convenient for them

● the inclusion of bought quality reflects the fact that buyers don't just buy a product or service, they also buy the quality process that has gone into its preparation

● bought process signifies again that buyers don't just buy a product, they also buy into a production or back-room operations process which has produced the product or service.

In the rest of this chapter, we'll look at each of the elements of the buyer relationship framework in more detail and then link them back to the key marketing objectives and strategies mentioned in chapter five.

buyer management

Buyer management has to do with the handling of relationships with buyers and management of buyer accounts. Whereas segmentation, targeting and positioning have established the scenario, buyer management is about the whole process of interaction with prospects and buyers.

The marketing function within your company

We've already discussed the importance of communication and to that effect everybody within your organization is a part of the marketing function. Some of the key players are:

- *Salesman/woman* – this person is the 'door opener'. He or she initiates the contact as directed by the management's marketing strategy. The person project-manages individual selling processes.

- *Marketing/Sales Director* – oversees the implementation of the sales and marketing strategy.

- *Managing Director* – ensures that the sales and marketing strategy is producing profits.

- *Receptionist* – every incoming call or visitor is greeted courteously and treated with efficiency.

- *Technical Manager* – provides the technical input required to ensure that the product reaches the requirements of the buyer. Liaises with the buyer's technical department.

- *Quality Manager* – initiates the quality procedures that'll be required to ensure that the product meets the expectations of the buyer. Liaises with the buyer's quality department.

The above will vary from company to company and sector to sector, but they're all key players in ensuring a successful marketing programme.

Whether you're supplying a product or service the success of your marketing is in the hands of every employee within your organization. Anyone who thinks that they're not a part of the marketing process needs to be re-educated!

Attitude

The first decision for buyer management is: what's the basic attitude to buyers going to be? This'll be the attitude that informs the actions of all co-workers to prospects and buyers.

One possible attitude is that the buyer is king and is always right. Whatever he or she says goes. We'll stand on our heads for him or her. Another possible attitude is that buyer relationships are important to the growth, strength and security of our business, but we'll choose the buyers we work with. When the company decides to work with a buyer, it'll be on the basis of mutual respect. If the relationship is to be a partnership, it must work two ways. Openness is not one-sided. A profit opportunity must exist for both sides. We prefer the second of the above two attitudes!

Values

Buyer management needs to have certain values which shine through in the relationship:

- commitment
- a willingness to share financial risk
- long-term perspective
- openness
- honesty
- reliability
- room to make mistakes
- genuine profit opportunity for both
- active working on each other's behalf
- flexibility.

Resources

The company should decide a strategy for the commitment of resources to any buyer relationship. This means setting standards for the level of service to be provided. Service includes technical support, training, after-sales support and systems support.

A key aspect of resource usage in business-to business marketing is team selling. This means everyone whose job affects the buyer's account is involved in the sales team, whether it's the driver, the accounts clerk, the chief executive or the professional sales executives.

Of course, the key resource at managerial level is time. Later, we'll be introducing a way of analyzing key accounts. This analysis can be used to focus management and executive time on the accounts which have the greatest potential for profit.

Budgeting of capital and current expenditure is a key part of buyer management. This is the area of the buyer relationship management framework which acts as a focus for setting budgets, for drawing up the action plans for each other aspect of the mix, and for actively seeking and monitoring feedback on progress, in terms of figures or qualitative achievements against the key objectives of buyer recruitment and buyer retention.

PARTNERSHIP DEVELOPMENT

It was mentioned in chapter two, that if the purchasing professional of today is into partnership sourcing, shouldn't the sales and marketing professional of today be into partnership development? If he or she is working to an open and honest framework, to develop win-win type situations, then shouldn't sales/marketers be working in the same manner to achieve the same goal? Shouldn't they be asking the same kind of questions that the buyer is asking? If securing business is going to cost more in financial terms, is it not about time that these so-called partnership arrangements move forward and become true partnerships?

So, hasn't partnership sourcing created the true partnerships that were imagined? Yes it has, in cases where buyers have tried to initiate a stronger link between companies. Where partnerships have struggled and failed to be true partnerships is where the marketer has allowed the matter to rest. It's no use bemoaning the fact that you've won a contract, told the buyer everything and are now having to reduce costs further. Question if you want the business, and know the buyer's company inside out. What are its future plans? Is there increasing potential for you and your business? Do you wish to be associated with the company? Did you really know what you were getting into?

The idea of partnership development is that everything is analyzed up front, decisions made early, and marketers' openness reciprocated by the buyer's openness. Its aim is to ensure that there'll be no future surprises – that you know the buyer's needs now and how they'll change in the future and that you know the buyer's company almost as well as he or she does.

By positioning yourselves in this manner you can then work more constructively with buyers. You can be pro-active and make their jobs easier and in turn make your job easier. You cement the relationship and can more strongly lock out your competitors.

Before partnership development can work, you have to ensure that your own company has an open and honest approach in the information it supplies to buyers. You have to have a clear understanding of your cost structures and strategy. You have to have taken the market apart and be focused in your objectives. Without these elements you're shooting in the dark and endangering the future health of your company. Then you have to be prepared to reveal all.

The key to partnership development is communication. This is communication at several levels and as a continous process. The importance of communication cannot be understated. Have you ever made a quote then neglected to follow it up? Most people have. Poor communication in today's age of advanced communication technologies is unforgivable. Manage your communication agenda. Another aspect of poor communication is how many opportunities have you missed? How many orders could you have received? Don't be a part of poor communication. Invest in technology, use diaries, year planners and computerized contact report systems. Ensure that you and your company aren't subject to poor communications.

TRICKS OF THE TRADE

Within partnership development it's essential that everyone knows who your key buyers are. They should understand the business that they're in and the products that you'll be supplying. Your company should be comfortable in dealing with the buyer at all levels. If you have direct lines, make these available so that your customer can receive direct attention. When buyers visit your plant have as much of the management involved as possible. Give them as much attention as possible. Make them feel important and take the opportunity to make your own staff feel important by formal and informal introductions to staff at all levels within your company. Every contact made during the visit is a marketing tool – use it to your advantage.

Internal communications

Partnership sourcing and development can only truly work where internal communication is at a good level. Be certain to audit your internal communication techniques. Are all those people who may need to know about a particular project aware of the project? How was it communicated? When we say 'all those people', we're talking about everybody who'll be involved on that project and everyone who may have some form of contact with the buying company.

Test your internal communications out. Talk to the receptionist, the project engineer, the quality manager, the quality inspector, the SQA engineer, the purchasing people, the logistics manager and the directors. Do they all know about your latest project and who the buyer is?

When making the initial contact and follow-up the aim is to sell the benefit of your company's products/services. A second element is gleaning information from the buyer about his or her company, its sourcing criteria, amount of goods/services procured, and which of your competitors it buys from and why.

In partnership sourcing the buyer obtains the information that he or she requires though a form-filling process, i.e. the quotation support forms and the supplier information/self-assessment forms. In partnership development the marketer asks for this openness to be reciprocated by asking the buyer to complete a form. This form should be issued either with a quotation or following a quotation. It should seek to identify all of those key areas that give a good picture of the company and enable you to estimate the potential worth of this account to you. It allows you to decide how much time and energy to devote in securing the business and whether or not you wish to be aligned with such a company.

A plastics company could use a form like the example overleaf. Once completed, this buyer profile form provides much of the information that you eventually would've gained through visits to and discussions with the buyer and various personnel within the company. On the above form it may be that the total spend on plastics is $100,000 divided between four suppliers. Rather than become a fifth supplier you may then take the decision that you no longer wish to pursue this account, as your time and energy would be best served elsewhere. Alternatively, you may decide to go for an all or nothing approach and instigate a strategy to secure all the business.

The form may show a downward trend in turnover and decreasing profits with a stable number of employees. This may lead you to decide that you don't wish to be involved with a company on a downward spiral. The required frequency of deliveries may be higher than anticipated and this will lead you to review your delivery costs. If buyers require FMEAs, it would be prudent to discuss with the quality personnel what problems have been encountered with the product you are quoting on. An additional trimming operation that wasn't originally envisaged may become evident.

The key element of all these factors is that they affect the cost to you of dealing with that company. From this base you can make decisions with confidence and based on facts.

Buyer profile – to be completed by all new and potential customers

Company Name:

	199	199	199
Turnover			
No. of employees:			

Address:

Telephone number:

Fax number:

Manufacturers of:

Other plant locations:

Key contacts

Purchasing	
Quality	
Engineering	

Purchasing policy

Do you operate a global sourcing policy?	Y/N
Do you practice partnership sourcing?	Y/N
Do you require supplies on a JIT basis?	Y/N
If so, state frequency of delivery generally required	per week
Do you produce plastic mouldings in house?	Y/N

If so, what are your criteria for selecting components to produce in house and for those that you subcontract?

What is your total spend on plastic mouldings from subcontractors?	per annum
How many subcontractors do you have for plastic mouldings?	
Do you pass tooling costs on to your customers?	Y/N

Quality policy

Do you operate a supplier grading programme?	Y/N
Do you require SPC?	Y/N
Do you require FMEAs?	Y/N
Do you have a supplier quality procedure document?	Y/N
Do you have a defined initial samples submission procedure?	Y/N

Engineering policy

Do you require engineering and technical support on new projects?	Y/N
If yes, is there a requirement for CAD facilities?	Y/N

Please return together with company brochure and supplier quality procedures/manuals to The Sales Manager, Plastic Company Ltd., The Arbours, Birmingham

Buyers make their decisions and long-term commitments based on facts and information that they receive from you. In the past, too often marketers' decisions were made on thankfulness for the contract and a few facts collated from sporadic market research. Now is the time for marketers to pick and choose who they supply, based on structured market research, focused marketing activity and up-front knowledge of the potential buyer.

BUYER ASSESSMENT

As highlighted in 'Buyers' Expectations' in chapter four, you as the marketer are continually being assessed. It's important that you also maintain an assessment of your customers. Too many people don't know which accounts represent the bulk of their sales or have the best potential for developing future business, or are problem accounts that issue poor schedules, pay late and require continual additional support in one shape or another.

TRICKS OF THE TRADE

○ *Having a structured approach to buyer assessment allows you to devote resources to the right areas, and to make decisions based on sound judgement and facts.*

○ *Continual buyer assessment will protect your margins, ensure extra activity is not unaccounted for and allow you to practise a true partnership relationship with your buyers.*

The buyer profile form provides a number of key points that allows initial assessment. Thereafter, a procedure to monitor a buyer's performance needs to be implemented. This could take into consideration such items as schedule performance, responsiveness to queries, volumes as per original quotation and payment according to terms. By continual assessment, buyers ensure that their companies are aligned only with those suppliers that can best meet their needs and fulfil their criteria.

In partnership development an assessment programme should be operated that allows for the monitoring of a buyer's performance. This performance can be linked to a grading system so that key accounts can be easily identified. It enables accounts with good potential to be identified and provides evidence on which buyers are best delisted. An example of the type of form to be used is given overleaf. Obviously the form should be tailored to suit your particular needs and business sector. It should involve information from a number of departments and give a broad picture of the relationship and business that exist with a particular buyer. The form should be designed in a simple format that allows for ease of completion and interpretation. With this example the buyer is being assessed against six parameters:

- schedules

- deliveries

- volumes

- payments

- business development

- others.

The first four parameters have a bearing on both immediate and short-term costs, whereas the fifth parameter relates to potential short- and long-term gains to be made. The sixth parameter assists in the assessment of your long-term strategy in relation to the buyer.

Schedules

For busy manufacturing companies good scheduling is of vital importance. Good schedules enable production planning to be effective and efficient. It reduces the down time of machines and minimizes the changing of tools to accommodate the production of different components.

WATCH OUT!

Last-minute changes to schedules that are poorly communicated put you in difficulties. Production has to be interrupted, replanned and possibly affects your own sourcing, as additional materials have to be bought in at short notice. All this costs you money. Buyers with very poor schedules and several last-minute variations are expensive to keep and serve. It's in their interest to maintain you as a cost-effective supplier, therefore they should be open to you working with them to help resolve the problem. Maybe they don't see a problem. The buyer assessment form would at least make it clear to you that there's a problem. How you handle it from there is down to you, but if you choose to ignore it don't be surprised if the problem exacerbates itself rather than fades away. Remember, it's costing you money.

Buyer assessment form

Name of company: ────────────────────────────────

Location(s): ────────────────────────────────────

Account no.: ─────────────────────────────────────

Value of supplies: ───────────────────────────────
(last 3 years)

Date of first supply: ────────────────────────────

1 Schedules	A	Pts.	B	Pts.	C	Pts.
1.1 Are 3-monthly schedules issued?	on time	2	1 week late	1	more than 1 week late	0
1.2 Are forthnightly schedules issued?	on time	2	1 day late	1	more than 1 day late	0
1.3 Variance between monthly and fortnightly schedules	zero	10	1–15%	2	more than 15%	0
IF ANSWERED B OR C, INVESTIGATE AND REPORT:						
1.4 Are variations made on goods for delivery in:	4 weeks	2	1 week	1	less than 1 week	0
1.5 What percentage of total production do these variations represent?	5%	2	15%	1	more than 15%	0
1.6 How are variations to schedules made?	fax and/or phone	2	either fax, letter or phone	1	phone	0

2 Deliveries	A	Pts.	B	Pts.	C	Pts.
2.1 Are more deliveries having to be made than originally planned?	no	10	one extra per month	4	more than one a month	1
IF ANSWERED B OR C, INVESTIGATE AND REPORT:						
2.2 Are extra deliveries required because:	volumes are increasing	2	occasional last minute variations to schedules	1	too many last minute variations to schedules	0
2.3 Do the extra deliveries require another party to carry out the delivery?	no	2	sometimes	1	yes	0
2.4 Can the cost of these extra deliveries be passed on to the customer?	yes	2	sometimes	1	never	0

3 Volume	A	Pts.	B	Pts.	C	Pts.
3.1 Are volumes as per original quotation?	yes	11	no, higher	10	no, lower	0
IF ANSWERED B or C, INVESTIGATE AND REPORT:						
3.2 How much notice was given of an increase/decrease in volumes?	12 weeks	2	4 weeks	1	less than 4 weeks	0
3.3 Have we received satisfactory information to explain why there's been an increase/decrease in volumes?	yes	2	50% satisfied	1	no	0
3.4 Did we have to initiate communication to receive information?	no	2		–	yes	0
3.5 Are we satisfied in the level of communication that we've received?	yes	2	50% satisfied	1	no	0

4 Payments	A	Pts.	B	Pts.	C	Pts.
4.1 Are payments made to agreed terms?	yes within 30 days	5	no within 60 days	4	no more than 60 days	0
4.2 Are invoices queried?	never	5	sometimes	1	always	0
IF ANSWERED B OR C, INVESTIGATE AND REPORT:						
4.3 Are invoice queries delaying payments?	never	2	sometimes	1	always	0
4.4 Whos's at fault?	we are	2	both parties	1	they are	0

Buyer assessment form (continued)

5 Business development

5.1	Are we:	sole supplier	5	one of 2/3 suppliers	3	one of more than 3 suppliers	1
5.2	What proportion of business do we have?	100%	5	70–99%	4	less than 70%	1
5.3	What proportion of our business is with them?	70–100%	2	30–70%	1	less than 30%	
5.4	Have we received more or fewer quotation opportunities than expected?	more	2	as expected	1	less	0
5.5	Are we involved in any of their new projects?	yes, all of them	2	yes, a few	2	no, none at all	0
5.6	Do they have many new projects?	yes	2	a few	2	none	0
5.7	Are we being kept informed of new projects?	yes, always	2	sometimes	2	never	0
5.8	Is technical input required on:	new projects	2	existing projects	1	either	1
5.9	Are we expecting an increase/decrease in their business over the next 12 months?	increase	2	remaining stable	1	decrease	0
5.1	Where are increases arising from?	new and existing projects	2	new or existing projects	1	no increases	0
5.11	Where are decreases arising from?	no decreases	1	seasonal trends	0	a fall in their business	0

6 Others

6.1	Are they profitable?	yes	6	yes, though profits are low	3	no	0
6.2	Is the number of employees:	increasing	5	stable	2	decreasing	1
6.3	Are they part of a national/multinational group?	yes multinational	4	yes national	3	no	1
IF ANSWERED A OR B, INVESTIGATE AND REPORT:							
6.4	Is purchasing centralized?	yes	3	on some items	2	no	1
6.5	Is engineering centralized?	yes	3	on some items	2	no	1

Scores

1	Schedules	out of 14
2	Deliveries	out of 10
3	Volumes	out of 18
4	Payments	out of 10
5	Business development	out of 27
6	Others	out of 21

Total
out of 100

Grading

A   score between 90–100
     Key account, good relationship, very open, good business development opportunities
B   Score between 76–89
     Key account, potential for business development, increased openess and communication required
C   score between 51–75
     Potential key account, greater interaction between companies required
D   Score between 9–50
     Unless new account, justification required to maintain this account

Deliveries

Erratic scheduling can lead to erratic deliveries – another cost burden. Deliveries have to be planned and accounted for, with the costs being weighted into your prices. Sell competitively and your delivery cost element would have been calculated on a specific number of deliveries to be made and on the volumes involved. More deliveries result in increased costs. What has to be considered is where these additional deliveries are stemming from. More deliveries but lower volumes can become very expensive to support.

The buyer assessment form identifies where deliveries are becoming a cost burden and allows you to understand where the problem arises and how the costs are affecting your business. This enables you to address any problems with the buyer.

Volumes

Your original quotation was based on set volumes. These volumes will fluctuate at some point. What we need to assess is whether that fluctuation has cost us financially. Increasing volumes are generally a good thing, but if insufficient notice was given it may lead to production problems and poor delivery performance, which has affected how the buyer perceives your ability. Volumes may increase so dramatically that it's impossible for you to meet this increased demand.

The converse is obviously where volumes fall. This immediately affects your profitability. Certain costs will remain the same or be higher. For example, delivery costs per part may increase as you lose on the discounts that come from delivering parts en masse. There are other warning signs to look for in reducing volumes, and your relationship with your buyer should be strong enough for him or her to impart the precise explanation.

Payments

Payments are critical to your cash-flow. Too many companies making late payments could, potentially, put your own company in a difficult situation. The cost of borrowing is expensive and doesn't allow for an efficient operation. The cost of resolving invoice queries and ensuring payments are made to terms has to be considered. If there are recurring invoice problems this needs to be identified and resolved.

Business development

Here you try to identify the potential of a buyer. You need to be aware of where your business relationship could take you. This information is essential to your long-term strategy for each individual buyer and for your collective marketing approach. The business development opportunities, within a number of key buyer accounts, may throw up certain patterns or niche areas where you're developing a certain expertise.

All the other four parameters so far measured may indicate a poor account but, if there's a high score for business development, it may well be worthwhile investing in the relationship in order to realize the potential.

Others

This section looks at areas outside of your immediate relationship with the buyer. It aims to gain an overall picture of the buyer and allows you to ascertain the long-term worth and stability of the buyer. One of the first checks that a buyer will do is to check your company's financial stability. You should always have some record of your buyer's financial track record. You want to know if you'll get paid.

Grading system

By using these parameters you get a picture of the cost of the relationship in proportion to the current level of business and a perception of the future potential. By scoring the buyer on these parameters you can introduce a grading system, which should allow you to identify key accounts where the relationship is working. It should also indicate poor accounts where the relationship isn't working and where, in your company's best interests, the relationship is best dissolved.

Using this view of buyers we can identify where problems are and tackle those problems head on. This means that the problems don't remain buried deep in one department or another. It's very difficult to assess the cost of a buyer/supplier relationship. When a decision is taken to delist an account, it so often comes about as a result of decreasing volumes, falling opportunities with that account and a 'they've always been a problem account anyway' type of attitude. This doesn't highlight where the failings stem from, nor does it allow you to truly assess the potential worth of your account base.

Buyer assessment reveals details on your buyers but it also reveals the strength of your relationship with that buyer. Your company has a collective responsibility to maximize the profits and return from your investment in developing business. Only through assessing the buyer in a structured manner can you truly appreciate the success of your company in building and developing the relationship you and your company have.

Initially, it may prove prudent to carry out buyer assessments every three months, moving to every six months when a buyer has demonstrated a degree of grading stability. No buyer should be viewed as being above the assessment process. Indeed, your key buyers, who you have the best possible relationship with, should set the benchmark for all the other buyers.

Buyer assessment forms enable you to highlight areas where the relationship between you and your buyers requires attention. It may be that you opt to discuss the assessment with the buyer, using this opportunity to highlight weak areas of communication. However, you may feel that to openly discuss the assessment would jeopardize the relationship. There's no golden rule, so remember that buyer assessment is for your use and your benefit. Some buyers would view as very professional companies that take such a structured and constructive assessment of the supply/buyer relationship. Others may deem it unnecessary. The latter are more likely to come from companies that talk about but don't practice partnership sourcing. Use the assessment forms and grading system to help you manage your business better.

INTERNAL DOCUMENTATION

The buyer profile and buyer assessment forms are just two types of useful documentation that you could use. Nobody likes filling in forms, so records become incomplete and are rarely updated. Because working in partnership with your buyer is so dependent upon communication, your internal documentation should provide a complete picture of the buyer and the stage of the selling cycle that you are in. Without this you'll be working as individuals to satisfy the needs of the buyer. At some point the lack of information and communication will allow the door to open for mistakes and concessions. You'll be working reactively instead of pro-actively, at a disadvantage and struggling.

The essence of your internal control documentation is that everyone should feel comfortable with it. It's not the object of this book to advise on internal documentation, suffice to say it should be clear and concise, lending itself to ease of completion.

buyer need

Buyer need is what used to be called product or service. This is a way of focusing attention on what the product is supposed to do, namely fulfil the buyer's need. There are three levels of customer or buyer need:

- core benefit

- specified need

- additional need.

The core benefit is the essential problem that the product solves for the buyer, e.g. guaranteed safety of an aerospace component or lowest cost casting design. The specified need is what the buying organization actually specifies in terms of features, tolerances and performance. The additional needs are all of the extra services and back-up the buyer expects. All of these levels of need come together to form the total requirement. It's essential to have worked out the three different levels for your organization's offering.

PRODUCT AND PROCESS INNOVATION

As we've seen in chapter five, innovation is one of the four main marketing strategies, a vital way of retaining buyer accounts. In the past, the phrase 'new product development' was adequate to describe this strategy. Nowadays, however, in business-to-business marketing, changes in product are frequently accompanied by changes in the back room or manufacturing processes of both the supplier and the purchaser. Process innovation and product or service innovation go hand in hand. The operations process and the new product need to be engineered simultaneously, to ensure hitch-free service introduction or product build.

A close relationship between supplier and buyer reduces the risk of new product failure. The existence of the relationship also gives the supplier the inside track on the purchasing organization's new projects. In that respect, much innovation is buyer-led, i.e. it arises directly from the buyer's need for a new solution to a business problem.

The degree of innovation can vary from a truly inventive idea with which the supplier is first to market, to a cheaper copy of what the market leader has done, or a new application of long-established technology to a different sector.

Increasingly, innovation is becoming time-driven as firms strive to get

EXAMPLE

Some buyers need a process not a product

Sheppard Moscow is an international consultancy, specializing in organizational development. It has offices in the UK and mainland Europe and works with a wide range of clients, including Schering, Shell, United Distillers, Bankers Trust, Safeway and Lloyds Bank, to build their capability to implement strategic change through people. This involves the management of cultural change, empowerment and teamworking.

Michael Nolan has been a consultant with Sheppard Moscow since 1992 and was previously with Amdahl. He makes a number of points about the relationship between product and process in business-to-business consulting. For example, in terms of engaging clients, the key communications medium is word of mouth. A human resource director or business development manager will hear from his or her peers in other operations 'on the grapevine' how Sheppard Moscow added value to its operations, carrying out a successful assignment for them in, say, managing cultural change. The prospective client may call the consultancy when pro-actively seeking to shortlist consultants for a project, or, if Michael calls the client, the client will often have heard by word of mouth. Expensive brochures, flyers and videos speak nowhere near as loudly as an excellent assignment for a satisfied client.

So word of mouth and track record will help greatly to secure a face-to-face meeting with a client in this business. But the next issue is: what are you going to offer or 'sell' the client? Consultancy is about process, not a product. Some firms have templates or standard services, which they try to adapt to their different clients' situations and requirements. But in order to be capable of working with world-class organizations which are making significant changes in the way they do business, it is essential to think process and relationship, not product or service.

If Michael says to a client, relying on track record, 'We did an excellent job for X', the 'client' will respond, 'We're not like X; we do things differently here'. So the consultant cannot formulate the product until he draws out the client's situation and requirements. He'll probably respond: 'We recognize you're different. We haven't worked with your company before on this particular kind of project, but we've the flexibility and process management skills to make it happen. Besides, we thrive on challenges!'

Consultants cannot afford to become absorbed with their 'product' or 'service', because they don't know what the next client project will require. The client's need is for a relationship based on process. ○

their new offerings to the market quicker than the competitors. Also, cross-functional teams are now the norm. It's essential that a holistic view is maintained of the development process. This requires the involvement of people with many different perspectives on the new offering, including marketing, sales, engineering, quality assurance, operations, purchasing, the legal department and logistics.

INNOVATION PROCESS

Traditionally, innovation models illustrate a multi-stage process as follows:

- idea generation

- idea screening

- concept testing

- business analysis

- product or service development

- market testing

- commercialization.

RISK AND COMPETITION

The size of the innovation investment, however, and the closeness of competitors, will dictate the way the innovation is developed. If there are lots of competitors and the investment is relatively small, the risk involved in not doing it, and of not doing it quickly, is greater than the risk of doing it. In that situation, a major effort will be necessary.

If the innovation investment is large and there are very few competitors around with the capability to beat the company to market, a more leisurely pace can be adopted and more time devoted to getting it right.

FAST TRACK

Because innovation should be buyer-led doesn't mean that the initiative should always lie with the other side. Buyers like pro-active suppliers that can exceed their expectations and work out ways to save cost or improve design and service before they're asked.

NO NEED FOR PERFECTION

Innovation doesn't have to be perfect. If a company waits for the perfect solution, it runs an increasing risk that a competitor will beat it to market with an acceptable innovation which isn't as good, or as technically 'sound', but may be perfectly saleable. The advantage of getting into the market first with something, even if it's not perfect, is that the buyers who are prepared to work with that solution provide an immensely useful feedback source for further developments.

TOTAL FRAMEWORK, NOT JUST PRODUCT OR SERVICE

Another point about innovation is that it doesn't have to be about product or service alone. It can come from any element of the framework. For example, in the area of buyer communications, a supplier could add an EDI capability, even if buyers aren't pressing for it. This is a small 'innovation' in the buyer relationship which improves the communications capability. Or again, the supplier could decide to introduce a quality system into its operational process. This isn't part of the product as such, being another element in the buyer relationship management framework, but most definitely has a profound effect on it.

buyer cost

Buyer cost is a repositioning of the term 'price' in order to look at it from the point of view of the buyer.

PRICING OBJECTIVES AND STRATEGIES

The pricing objective is to win the business at least cost to the company with the greatest margin possible.

In business-to-business marketing, costing of products is a critical skill, which directly affects margin. This skill is ineffective if the company's cost base is out of line. This can happen if the company is smaller than its competitors and carries a higher unit fixed cost, or if it cannot command the same or lower prices than its competitors for its inputs, whether these be money, people or materials.

COST REDUCTION Nowadays, many purchasers expect annual reductions in the cost of the services and products they buy in. The answer to this is to pre-empt them. This requires recognition of the major contribution that design can play in cost control. The following diagram illustrates the relative significance of design, labour, material and overhead in terms of cost.

Who casts the biggest shadow?

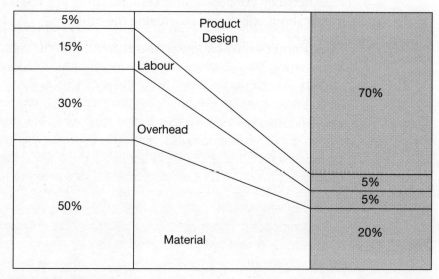

Source: FKI Automotive

YIELD IMPROVEMENT Another way to achieve cost reduction is to improve yield, reduce scrap and rework costs. Some industries, such as ceramic core production, can have yield rates of as low as 65 per cent on some product lines.

buyer convenience

This is a reframing of 'distribution'. It's a useful way to remind ourselves that the goal of the distribution effort is to make things convenient for the buyer. Buyers wants things when they want them and where they want them.

A review should be carried out of what buyers' expectations are in relation to delivery and what resources the company has to comply with them.

buyer information and communications

This used to be called 'promotion' in the old 'marketing mix'. The new name enables a broader scope to be considered. In the past, marketing research and promotion were frequently discussed separately, being separate activities carried out by two quite different types of people (i.e. market researchers and advertising people). However, the links between communication and information are so close it's crazy to talk about one without including the other.

Cynics won't express surprise at this schizophrenic split. After all, for many years, lots of companies have gathered information without actually using it to communicate, and there are lots of people who like to communicate without conveying any information – especially in sales and marketing.

Another split in the thinking about communication is that promotion is usually seen as the selling company talking to the purchaser. Because everyone wants to be heard above the noise of the competition, they shout as loud as they can. From the buyer's point of view, it's like trying to buy handcrafts in a tourist market – there are so many people calling out to you it's hard to focus on simply getting your requirements met!

If promotion is talking to (or, more usually, *at*) the buyer, marketing research is listening to the buyer. Both come under the umbrella of buyer communications. Research is simply inbound communications, the rest is outbound.

BUYER INFORMATION SYSTEM

Every organization which is serious about its business-to-business marketing has got to have a buyer information system (BIS). This means a computer database containing all relevant information on buyers and prospects. We live in the age of information technology. Information is readily available and the technology exists to handle it. A successful marriage of the two in a buyer information system can yield incredibly productive insights for your company.

With the proliferation of software packages and hardware solutions, it may seem difficult to design a configuration that works. There can be all sorts of problems about 'getting the computers to talk to each other'. There are issues about software portability and system connectivity. Nowadays, however, most of these problems are disappearing. It should now be possible to combine in one set of related files or records all data relating to a particular organization, whether an existing buyer, a prospect or a competitor. The information can include free text information (e.g. a competitor's financial statements scanned in from hard copy) or a relationship history (read in electronically from the accounts payable records).

SOURCES OF INFORMATION

The BIS should be fed from all the available sources of information. We're not just talking about newspaper reports and financial statements here. Every contact between buyer and product or service provider is a potential source of information. In other words, the source isn't just the person, it's the event or the contact. Any contact between buyer and seller involves exchange of information.

Examples of sources of

Here are some ways in which information can be exchanged between buyer and seller:

- marketing research

- personal selling

- corporate/product/service brochures

- product/packaging

- promotional give-aways

- training materials/courses

- advertising

- sponsorship

- direct mail

- service call-outs

- deliveries

- exhibitions

- media relations

- quotations

- invoicing and statements of account

- factory visits

- EDI

- e-mail

- telephone answering

- complaint handling

- signage

- company vehicles

- billboards

- posters

- focus groups

- surveys (phone, mail)

- letters.

Communication needs to be defined this widely in order that management becomes or is aware of its scope for good – or evil!

TWO-WAY INFORMATION FLOW

It's important to grasp the difference between a communications opportunity and what you use it for – inbound or outbound communication. All of these opportunities are two-way. Messages can be transmitted or received by the company. A factory visit from a key buyer is a powerful opportunity to sell the company; but it's also an opportunity to do market research. A prospecting exercise, e.g. by phoning around a number of companies in a potential new market to get information, is also a way of giving information about the company.

Remember that a buyer is making judgements all the time about your company, some rational, some non-rational. If the company has a consistent, systematic and thorough grasp of its communications opportunities, it'll be successful in communicating with its customers and prospects.

COMMUNICATIONS AND CREATIVITY

If you consider business-to-business manufacturers and service providers, it's difficult to get excited about the creativity of their advertising. The manufacturers tend to be obsessed with technical copy and the services people just seem to have difficulty coming up with any kind of catchy, successful concept at all!

There's a reluctance among sellers to get involved with creative agencies. This is caused principally by four factors:

● meanness (the aversion to marketing investment which is endemic in business-to-business markets)

● arrogance ('I could just as easily think up a slogan for my company as some jerk in an ad agency')

● group myopia ('If we all sit down together, I'm sure we can all come up with an exciting mission statement')

● ignorance (the lack of awareness of contemporary advertising and communications techniques and refusal to believe they could be worth discussing).

The result? The company has a default communications strategy. In other words, instead of being seen as a go-ahead, up-to-date confident organization, it's regarded as a shambolic collection of amateurs.

FAST TRACK

Image matters. Image is at least 50 per cent of business. If a company doesn't pro-actively make a distinctive image for itself, other people, i.e. its competitors, will make one for them! The best way to make an image is to hire a creative agency and let the experienced specialists do it.

BRANDING

This is commonly seen as a subject which has to do with consumer products, but there's no reason why it couldn't or shouldn't be used for business products and services. A distinctive, credible and clear brand can help to focus the minds of the co-workers as well as the buyers on the core attributes of the organization. It also helps buyers to distinguish the company from its competitors.

Branding opportunities are as numerous as communication opportunities and contacts. Once the brand values, positioning statement, logo and slogan or strapline have been developed in line with the segmentation, targeting and positioning process, every opportunity should be used to communicate the brand, from sales presentations to delivery truck liveries, to print ads in the specialist magazines.

The really important point to grasp about branding, however, is that the brand has a strategic value, not just a communications value. It has a strategic value because it helps to position the organization in its target segments against its competitors.

PERSONAL SELLING
Initial contact

The initial contact that you choose to make with a prospect will either be by phone or via a letter, probably accompanied with a brochure. This is the first time that the buyer has an opportunity to form an impression of your company. A clear, concise message has to be conveyed that secures the attention of the buyer. A 40-page brochure that 'outlines' the capability of your company is unlikely to be read. In fact, a 40-page brochure may indicate to the buyer that here's a company willing to spend a lot of money on something which is of little benefit – a wasteful company.

Think of the mailshots that you've received and those that have held your attention. Some come through the post and have so many different parts to them that you're not sure which part to refer to first, and which part will outline what the mailshot is all about. What happens to these mail shots? They end up in file 13 – the bin.

The other thing that happens with company brochures is that they go out of date. This gives a wrong impression to the buyer and either misleads the buyer, who then becomes very disappointed and disillusioned in your company, or means the buyer isn't fully aware of your capability and chooses to ignore you, making your job all the harder.

The approach to making the initial contact is a personal choice. Some people like to send a brochure then make contact by phone, others prefer to call first and then send a brochure. How buyers respond is down to their own personality. Some will talk quite happily on the phone, without having the benefit of the company brochure, whereas others prefer to have the brochure first, before discussing anything at all. Choose the technique that you feel more comfortable with.

Unfortunately, there are no 'tricks of the trade' to the initial contact procedure, but the key rule is that, whether writing or telephoning, make sure that you're addressing the right individual and avoid, at all

costs, simply addressing mailshots to the 'Purchasing Manager'. Get the right name and use it. Be courteous, polite and concise.

With the initial contact, the aim is to secure a meeting that will afford you more time to sell the benefits of your company, product and/or service. It's important that whatever is discussed, in the initial stages, leaves the door open to future discussions. Bear in mind that the initial contact stage may take several phone calls and more than one form of written correspondence.

Persistence

Too many sales and marketing personnel are disheartened by that feeling of getting nowhere. They've called a prospect five times and each time the buyer has been non-committal to everything that's been suggested or proposed. Don't be put off. Another quick call to the buyer, in say a month's time won't cost you much in time.

One salesman once took 16 phone calls to secure his first appointment with a company. He knows it was 16 because he meticulously logged every call in his diary. He was persistent, and as so often happens his persistence was rewarded.

In business-to-business marketing there are so many factors that affect buyers in their role that they cannot deal with every prospective call, query or request immediately. Through persistence there'll always be some reward. It may not be a new contract, but it may be some very relevant market information that you were unaware of. Either way, professional persistence is long-term marketing, which ensures that the prospective buyer knows about your company.

What are we trying to achieve with the initial contact? We're trying to gain access to the buyer and his or her company. During our contact with the buyer, we should begin to build a rapport and have something new to say, each time we establish contact. One of the beauties of being concise is that you're able to expand upon various points and issues, not only as and when the need arises, but also when it suits you. By giving snippets of information, you're always leaving room to impart more information to the buyer. This gives you more reason to stay in touch. Through more conversation, you learn more about what the buyer is looking for.

Work with buyers to try and identify reasons why they should see you. They may be operating a global sourcing policy – so they're unable to select a supplier until they've acquired a substantial knowledge of the sources available. You're one of those suppliers, so without all the relevant information regarding your company buyers cannot, therefore, make a sound decision. They may have a preferred supplier list – how do they know that you're not better than them? They don't. Now this leads us back to taking the market apart. You know your strengths, you know your competitors', weaknesses, and you know which benefits to focus on. It may be that the buyer is working, primarily, on a project that's unrelated to your products. Take recognition of this, but ask when you should call, and ask when it would be appropriate to send the brochure. Very few buyers will turn round and give a point blank never. After all, it's not in their interest, they don't know what they're missing.

Most companies in the business-to-business market have to be able to identify all of the key potential suppliers. Without this they can never be sure if they're buying from the right people. Many people are nervous when it comes to making the initial contact. If you've taken the market apart and been ruthless in assessing your own advantages and disadvantages, then developing a confident strategy will be all the more easy. Having identified and decided upon your strategy, implementation should then take place with the utmost of confidence. A well-focused strategy based upon your strengths gives a company confidence to move forward and develop its market.

Sales call reluctance

You have a salesman who seems to do very little prospecting and who's starting to get left behind by his colleagues. So, you bring him into the office and give him a warning that, if he doesn't improve soon, you'll be left with no alternative but to fire him. He leaves your office with his self-confidence drained and his pride battered. Four weeks later you fire him, as he appears to have lost all interest. This has cost you money. You're going to have to recruit and train somebody and you're going to have to try to make up lost time yourself.

Sales call reluctance is a state of mind that hinders the salesperson from effective prospecting. Many senior management personnel aren't aware of or choose to ignore sales call reluctance. How many excellent sales people have been discarded due to a lack of understanding? In their excellent book *Earning What You're Worth? The Psychology of Sales Call Reluctance*, George W. Dudley and Shannon L. Goodson have identified 12 'faces' of call reluctance and also address call reluctance impostors such as low motivation. The following are examples of some of the faces of call reluctance:

- *Yielder* – this is someone who fears intruding on people and is overly polite, to avoid offending anyone, and indecisive. This person lacks assertiveness and will consider aggressiveness within sales as unprofessional and concentrate his or her efforts on sales through rapport building. The yielder is the most frequent type of sales call reluctance.

- *Hyper-pro* – this person is obsessed with his or her image. Hair, clothes, car and all aspects of appearance are critical to this person. These perfectionists are out to project an image that they are very successful.

- *Over-preparation* – here we have someone who continually analyzes and prepares for meetings and presentations and then re-analyzes and prepares. This person ends up doing very little. Generally, he or she displays little emotion and has a lifeless presentation style full of facts and information.

- *Doomsayer* – this person expects the worst and highlights, to himself or herself, all that could go wrong. The person is unable to cope with spontaneity, likes to follow a rigid sales presentation style, and becomes disoriented when a prospect interjects with something that he or she was not prepared for.

- *Stage fright* – this is someone who fears making group presentations, is generally, anxious about his or her appearance and will often try to cope by producing overpractised presentations.

- *Telephobia* – this is a fear of using the telephone for prospecting. Telephobic people need to psych themselves up in preparation for telephone prospecting and then are immediately deflated as soon as they're turned down.

- *Oppositional reflex* – here we have people who strive to appear complete and independent, and continually challenge everything. They believe that they always know better and are likely to explode if told otherwise. They are unreceptive to training and never learn, because they never listen, how to prospect successfully.

Other forms of sales call reluctance include role rejection, social self-consciousness, emotionally emancipated, referral aversion and separationist.

Call reluctance, once identified, can be rectified through the right training. It has been highlighted as a relatively common problem that has been ignored for a long time. The aforementioned book provides a comprehensive insight into both the symptoms and effective counter measures.

Follow up

You've established contact by phone. You forward a brochure. You phone up six months later. The buyer doesn't recall your original call or the receipt of your brochure. So, you send another brochure and phone again six months later. You have an identical conversation. You send another brochure. This scenario should never happen, but it does. Why? Because things happen that distract you, priorities change, best-laid plans and strategies go astray, it takes six months to overcome sales call reluctance, you become engrossed in your latest sale, a new managing director is appointed that makes you lose your focus. Following up the initial contact, quotation and queries must be managed. Without the correct management buyers form a negative impression of your company. There's a lack of thoroughness and professionalism in the approach that reflects on the company.

**TRICKS OF
THE TRADE**

○ *Find a system that suits you to act as a reminder to phone companies. Make a note in your diary, on your PC, in your filofax, on your laptop. Use contact management software.*

○ *Develop a reminder system and stick to it, develop it and improve it.*

○ *When you initiate contact again, remind the buyer that it was his or her suggestion that you phone again in two weeks, one month or whatever was said. Again, this really is common sense but it has to be said because so many people fail to do the simple things in life.*

Exhibitions are an effective way of communicating with buyers, particularly in the early stages of new market development. They can also be a complete waste of money!

Making an exhibition

EXAMPLE

A multinational corporation was in the habit of taking space at a major US exhibition. Four corporate divisions had a presence on the same stand. The annual cost was over $500,000, everything included. For years, divisional executives pointed out that they knew all their buyers already and could pick up the phone and call them whenever they needed. In short, the exhibition was a waste of time, energy and money. Their mutterings were ignored, until there was a change of management at corporate level. The incoming chief executive took one look at the cost/benefit and killed the stand stone dead, right between the eyes.

If a company does decide to take a space at an exhibition, it should be aware that some buyers have a 'three-year guide to newcomers'. In the first year in which the new company is present, they simply note the fact that it's there. In the second year, they might notice it again and think to themselves: 'Well, they've not gone bust'. In the third year, they begin to think it might be worth talking to the newcomer.

That may be a wild generalization, but it contains two messages. Firstly, don't underestimate the amount of time it'll take to gain interest among buyers. Secondly, once a company takes a stand at an exhibition, failure to take space the following year sends a signal to buyers. They may conclude, rightly or wrongly, that the company is having financial difficulties, or cannot work out its communications programme.

Exhibition checklist If a company wishes to invest in an exhibition, this is the procedure:

● find a directory of exhibitions for the relevant market

● identify the relevant exhibitions – note the dates!

● call the exhibition organizers and ask for a visitor profile, space plan, cost schedule and proforma agreement

- choose a space that has good traffic flow

- use an agency to put together a stand design and develop some copy for the exhibition catalogue, newspapers and sector publications

- update the company brochures

- hire a photographer to take shots of the stand

- buy or develop a database of prospects and buyers to invite to the stand (make it interesting for them!)

- staff the stand with competent sales and technical people

- use the exhibition as an opportunity to research competitors, technological developments and selling opportunities

- capture and follow up all sales leads within one week.

DATABASE/DIRECT MARKETING

Effective use of database marketing is illustrated by a mailshot used by Siemens in support of a stand it had taken at a key communications exhibition. The show featured all of the latest products and services on offer in the rapidly expanding field of communications. All of the major suppliers in the market participated, and its attendance profile included both technical specifiers and general management from a wide range of organizations in the public and private sectors. The show was widely publicised in the media.

Siemens demonstrated the full range of its voice and data communications capabilities under the slogan 'Siemens – Networking People'. The targets for the mailshot were a selected group of 420 important decision-makers. Siemens wanted to get these people along to its stand in order to:

- establish their communication requirements

- demonstrate the range of communications solutions on offer

- arrange follow-up visits to prospects' facilities.

The communications strategy was to direct mail a personalized, eye-catching invitation card. To incentivize people to attend the stand, a Siemens S3 GSM mobile phone was offered as a prize in a draw into which all attending invitees were entered. Prospect records were extracted from Siemens' existing database and this list cleansed and updated by phone call ten days before the exhibition. A creative agency was hired to design the personalized invitation card. The concept featured a photograph of the S3 GSM telephone on the invitation with the name and organization of the invitee in the digital display area of the phone.

Maurice McMonagle, marketing consultant with Siemens, who managed this campaign, was delighted with the results. The combination of accurate prospect listing, incentivization and personalization of the invite meant that 32 per cent of those targeted came to the stand, providing Siemens with substantial extensive exposure to its target segment and a substantial number of valuable sales leads.

MARKETING RESEARCH

Marketing research has been thoroughly explored in chapter one – 'Taking the market apart'. Here it's sufficient to make the point that good buyer information is impossible without an extensive information gathering operation.

TELESALES SUPPORT

Telesales support is a cost-effective way of generating qualified leads. This can be done by company personnel or contracted to a specialist agency. The main benefit of telesales is the time it saves the field salespeople by generating qualified leads. Research has shown that if telesales is to produce those benefits, it should have staff dedicated to it for an extended period and preferably away from busy working areas. This helps the operative's concentration and rhythm and enables a high quantity of calls to be made. Giving the job to a receptionist or PA doesn't always produce consistent quality results.

FACTORY/SITE VISITS

These are critically important in selling the organization and in picking up information about buyers and their companies.

bought quality

Buyers don't just buy products; they effectively buy whatever quality system or process the supplier uses. Buyers need to be sure that they're buying quality. Uncorroborated assurances that the product is of good quality mean nothing. Evidence gathered during a site visit that demonstrates that the supplier has successfully implemented a quality system and that quality techniques (e.g. statistical process control) are in operation will be very important.

Every organization needs to put in place a suitable quality system. A quality system is basically a process that promotes quality in the company's operating processes. The more commonly known quality systems are TQM and Investors in People. Quality systems are simply ways of making quality work in an organization. It's better to have a careful approach to these tools, because if their introduction isn't handled carefully, it can lead to difficulties.

What's important isn't what the quality systems are called or which is the latest in fashion, but what actual changes they can effect in company operating procedures that give better quality of product and service. TQM is based on a thorough appraisal of culture, commitment, communication, systems, teams and tools. It's not within the scope of this book to explore this topic in detail, but its importance for the good management of buyer relationships is critical.

bought process

The buyer isn't just buying a product or service. He or she is also buying the process that produces the service or product. The production or operations process needs to be buyer-focused just as much as any other aspect of the company's activities. Aspects of operations which need to be examined for buyer focus include:

- equipment capability

- plant layout

- process category – batch, job, flow

- flexibility of process

- capacity

- product variety capability

- production build and schedules.

This completes our review of the buyer relationship framework, a comprehensive tool for managing buyer relationships. It also brings us to the end of this book!

DON'T FORGET!

Building buyer relationships

○ This book is based on the principle of 'know your customer'. We've looked in detail at the buying function, buyer power and the buyer expectations within the total business context.

○ A comprehensive framework for business planning, has been put forward as well as a guide to successful management of buyer relationships.

○ Whatever business you're in we hope that this book will help you to develop successful business relationships with professional buyers.

index

other titles in this series

key accounts are different KEN LANGDON

In every business from computers to cat food, key customers are expecting closer working relationships and are using fewer suppliers. In an increasingly competitive world, with tougher selling conditions, nobody can afford to ignore this. It is time to re-adjust your activities with key accounts. They are a market, not just a customer. You need to learn how to market and sell your products to them and make sure that they remain a key acount for *your* company.

This is not a strategy book. It is a solution to the challenges you face, a practical implementable plan to get you on track immediately.

ISBN   0273 61780 X   Price   £19.99

direct hit MERLIN STONE, DEREK DAVIES and ALISON BOND

Direct Marketing is an essential part of marketing. Any company that ignores direct marketing does so at its peril. It enables you to communicate with your customers to let them know you are there, ensure that your products fulfil their needs, receive valuable feedback, build up a database and develop long term loyalty.

This book is a no-nonsense practical tool kit which will enable you to launch a successful direct marketing campaign. It is essential reading for all organizations, in all industries, whatever their size.

ISBN   0273 61689 7   Price   £19.99

marketing plans ANGELA HATTON

The constant challenge every manager today faces is to put the customer at the heart of their business, whilst getting 'more from less' resources. The key to success lies in planning. Not the routine annual ritual of preparing documents which gather dust all year. Rather planning as a dynamic and continuous management activity. Plans which are easy to produce and practical to use.

This book presents you with a fresh insight into the value of planning. Not a theoretical thesis, but a hands on, planning made simple but effective approach.

ISBN   0273 61693 5   PRICE   £19.99

database marketing IAN LINTON

Have you ever wondered how Virgin know what paper you like to read and have it ready on your seat when you board your flight? Or how on earth can Marriot hotels keep track of the likes and dislikes of 5 million people, even down to their favourite room? Are these people psychics?

No, but they have learnt how powerful a marketing tool a database can be. Are you getting the most out of your database? This book shows you how to use the information you have to improve your performance and customer relations. If you want to have spot on marketing, which will wow your customers, this book will give you the know-how you need.

ISBN   0273 61179 8   Price   £19.99

Please note that all prices are subject to change.